The Political Power of Protest

This book demonstrates the direct influence that political protest behavior has on Congress, the presidency, and the Supreme Court, illustrating that protest is a form of democratic responsiveness that government officials have used, and continue to draw on, to implement federal policies. Focusing on racial and ethnic minority concerns, this book shows that the context of political protest has served as a signal for political preferences. As pro-minority rights behavior grew and anti-minority rights actions declined, politicians learned from minority protest and responded when they felt emboldened by stronger informational cues stemming from citizens' behavior, a theory referred to as the "information continuum." Given the influence that minority protest actions have wielded over national government, the book offers a powerful implication. Although the shift from protest to politics as a political strategy has opened the door for institutionalized political opportunity, racial and ethnic minorities have neglected a powerful tool to illustrate the inequalities that exist in contemporary society.

Daniel Q. Gillion is an assistant professor of political science at the University of Pennsylvania. His research interests focus on racial and ethnic politics, political behavior, public opinion, and the American presidency. Gillion's research has been published in several journals and books, including *Oxford Handbook of Political Behavior*, *Electoral Studies*, and *The Journal of Politics*. Before joining the University of Pennsylvania's faculty, he was the distinguished provost Fellow in the political science department at the University of Rochester, where he completed his PhD. He currently serves as the 2012–2014 Robert Wood Johnson Health Policy Scholar and the Ford Foundation Fellow at Harvard University.

Cambridge Studies in Contentious Politics

Titles in the Series

Ronald Aminzade et al., *Silence and Voice in the Study of Contentious Politics*
Javier Auyero, *Routine Politics and Violence in Argentina: The Gray Zone of State Power*
Clifford Bob, *The Marketing of Rebellion: Insurgents, Media, and International Activism*
Charles Brockett, *Political Movements and Violence in Central America*
Valerie Bunce and Sharon Wolchik, *Defeating Authoritarian Leaders in Postcommunist Countries*
Christian Davenport, *Media Bias, Perspective, and State Repression*
Gerald F. Davis, Doug McAdam, W. Richard Scott, and Mayer N. Zald, *Social Movements and Organization Theory*
Todd A. Eisenstadt, *Politics, Identity, and Mexico's Indigenous Rights Movements*
Daniel Q. Gillion, *The Political Power of Protest: Minority Activism and Shifts in Public Policy*

(continued after the index)

The Political Power of Protest

Minority Activism and Shifts in Public Policy

DANIEL Q. GILLION
University of Pennsylvania

CAMBRIDGE UNIVERSITY PRESS
Cambridge, New York, Melbourne, Madrid, Cape Town,
Singapore, São Paulo, Delhi, Mexico City

Cambridge University Press
32 Avenue of the Americas, New York, NY 10013-2473, USA

www.cambridge.org
Information on this title: www.cambridge.org/9781107657410

First published 2013

Printed in the United States of America

A catalog record for this publication is available from the British Library.

Library of Congress Cataloging in Publication data
Gillion, Daniel Q., 1979– author.
The political power of protest : minority activism and shifts in public policy / Daniel Q. Gillion, University of Pennsylvania.
pages cm. – (Cambridge studies in contentious politics)
Includes bibliographical references and index.
ISBN 978-1-107-03114-2 (hardback) – ISBN 978-1-107-65741-0 (paperback)
1. Protest movements–United States. 2. Political participation–United States. 3. Minorities–Civil rights–United States. I. Title.
HN57.G565 2013
303.6′1–dc23 2012033206

ISBN 978-1-107-03114-2 Hardback
ISBN 978-1-107-65741-0 Paperback

Contents

Figures

Tables

Preface

After the 2010 midterm elections, President Barack Obama acknowledged that his party had received a "shellacking." Sixty-four Democratic members in the House of Representatives lost their jobs, the Republicans picked up six additional seats in the Senate, and Speaker of the House Nancy Pelosi relinquished her position to the tearful Representative John Boehner who lay in the wake of the election aftermath. It was the worst midterm loss suffered by any political party since 1938.

Before Representative Boehner went to the podium to offer his first speech as Speaker, he placed a televised congratulatory call to Tea Party activists in Ohio and said to them, "I'll never let you down." To some, this moment confirmed what many had suspected: the antigovernmental Tea Party protests that had taken place over the previous two years were an influential part of electoral outcomes. The non-electoral actions of the Tea Party suggest a revitalization of protest behavior in the contemporary United States. Even in the international setting, protest activities, such as the revolution that occurred in early 2011 in Egypt, have forced the world to take notice of the monumental power of citizens' protest behavior.

I see these actions as being part of the political process that we recognize exists but grapple to understand why and how, or even if, protest behavior matters to federal politicians. In the United States, we have a rich history of protest from which to explore citizens' influence. And arguably, nowhere is this information more abundant than in the narrative of racial and ethnic minorities' pursuit of equality. I draw on this history to delve into the political consequences of minority protest and explore some broad questions in this book: Can minority protest change citizens' perceptions of the importance of race? Can it move congressional leaders to action? Can it shift the focus of the president of the United States? Can it impact the judicial behavior of the Supreme Court? As this encompassing work will show, the answer to these questions is often "yes." However, one-word answers do not suffice in explaining the convolution that exists in linking protest behavior to federal government actions. Minority protest has succeeded in influencing government when the social environment of protest behavior, both contentious and moderate, informed politicians of the importance of minority grievances not only in relation to other salient topics on the political agenda but also in comparison to competing protests on race-related issues.

This book does not initiate the dialogue for understanding the influence of political protest on government; I stand on the shoulders of many pioneers who have come before me and added a wealth of knowledge on this subject. Neither is this book the final word on understanding the policy success of protest activity, nor should it be. What this work does is expand our discussion of citizen activism to multiple national institutions in order to recognize the larger scope of protest's influence. In doing so, I set out to challenge the myopic perceptions that constrain our understanding of the impact of protest behavior to the fringes of American democracy, rendering it as inaudible noise largely ignored by those in the political arena. I look to move beyond this impasse and center protest activity at the heart of the democratic process that has engendered, and continues to beget, national governmental attention to racial and ethnic minority concerns.

Acknowledgments

There is an endless number of individuals who have affected this project, and I want to acknowledge several scholars. At the University of Rochester, the birthplace of this book's idea, there were many individuals who read the beginning stages of this manuscript, shaped my ideas in talks, and discussed the multiple analytical approaches to tackle this project. These individuals include David Carter, Kevin Clarke, Gerald Gamm, Hein Goemans, Gretchen Helmke, James Johnson, Stuart Jordan, Jeremy Kedziora, Fabiana Machado, Navine Murshid, Michael Peress, Matthew Platt, Bingham Powell, Lynda Powell, Adam Ramey, Yoji Sekiya, Curtis Signorino, Arthur Spirling, and Randall Stone. I am particularly grateful to Lawrence Rothenberg, Valeria Sinclair Chapman, and Jeffrey Allen Tucker who sat on my dissertation committee and established the foundation of this book project.

I owe many thanks to my colleagues at the University of Pennsylvania that commented on the manuscript and offered critical feedback that allowed the manuscript to further develop. I am very appreciative of the support I received from Eileen Doherty-Sil, Tulia Falleti, Avery Goldstein, Nancy Hirschmann, Michael Horowitz, John Lapinski, Matthew Levendusky, Julia Lynch, Edward Mansfield, Marc Meredith, and Diana Mutz. Many faculty members contributed through informal discussions and departmental forums.

Several individuals have served as mentors from afar, not only influencing my thought process with their own writings but also providing sage advice when I needed it most. I am eternally thankful to Frank Baumgartner, Andrea Campbell, Claudine Gay, Jennifer Hochschild, Vince Hutchings, Jane Junn, Taeku Lee, Paula McClain, Christopher Parker, Dianne Pinderhughes, Sarah Soule, Sidney Tarrow, Vesla Weaver, and Christopher Wlezian.

There are three individuals, however, whose influence and advice not only transformed my daily ramblings into sound ideas for this book, but who have also changed my worldview. For that I owe a debt of gratitude, which I will never be able to repay, to Fredrick Harris, Richard Niemi, and Rogers Smith.

Finally, I dedicate this book to the Gil-Lions, a word I use to refer to the Gillion family. The tenacity to pursue all my academic endeavors started with my family unit. In particular, I am grateful to my parents, Kenneth Sr. and Shirley Gillion, for their uncompromising academic expectations. I am also thankful of the social and political discourse they created at an early stage of my life among me and my seven siblings, Brionne, Kenny Jr., Zacchaeus, Darrance, Tocarra, Cyril, and Gerald. Without my parents' vision of success, I would have blindly wandered through life.

In the end, however, this book was only made possible by the advice, comments, criticism, support, and love that was offered by my coauthor of life, my wife Leah.

Introduction

On June 11, 1963, in a televised address from the Oval Office, President John F. Kennedy identified "a moral crisis" facing the United States:

> The fires of frustration and discord are burning in every city, North and South, where legal remedies are not at hand. Redress is sought in the streets, in demonstrations, parades, and protests, which create tensions and threaten violence and threaten lives. We face, therefore, a moral crisis as a country and as a people. It cannot be met by repressive police action. It cannot be left to increased demonstrations in the streets. It cannot be quieted by token moves or talk. It is time to act in the Congress, in your State and local legislative body and, above all, in all of our daily lives. (Kennedy 1964, 467)

With these fiery words, Kennedy created a defining moment for minority protesters. In the most public of fashions, the president acknowledged the plight of racial minorities and vowed to take executive action. It was no coincidence that the president's speech came on the heels of protests in Birmingham, Alabama, a city that had become a battleground for the civil rights movement earlier that year under the guidance of the Southern Christian Leadership Conference. By May 2, the demonstrations in Birmingham had grown so large that police officers resorted to using school buses and vans to transport protesters to overfilled jails. These protest activities, referred to as "Project C" for "confrontation," persisted for weeks and culminated in the infamous events of May 3, when the nation tuned into its television sets to see not disorderly adults being handcuffed, but teenagers cornered by police officers with trained canines and little girls huddled together to soften the unrelenting force of the water that was slamming their backs into concrete walls. The scene was disturbing.

Although other minority protest events had approached this level of violence, few found their way into the living rooms of the American public. The presence in Birmingham of several media outlets, both foreign and domestic, only exacerbated the cruelty of the racial clash playing out there. After watching the scenes from Birmingham on his own television screen, Kennedy sensed public opinion was shifting in favor of minority protestors – and he was right. In 1963, race relations became the most important problem facing the nation: more than 52 percent of Americans surveyed felt that addressing racial and ethnic minority concerns should be the government's number-one priority. This was a substantial increase from the 8 percent who had felt the same way only a year earlier.

To the government fell the simple question of what to do next. Kennedy's even simpler answer was "Act." Thus, he reversed his lackluster approach to race relations and proposed sweeping reform. On June 21, Kennedy implemented Executive Order 11114, which extended the authority of the President's Committee on Equal Employment Opportunity to end discrimination in employment as well as in governmental contracts with public and private organizations receiving federal financial assistance. On that same day, he sent a letter to Secretary of Defense Robert McNamara that urged the secretary to adhere to the recommendations of the Committee on Equal Opportunity in the Armed Forces, which stated that more must be done to improve the discriminatory practices suffered by black military personnel in both on-base and off-base environments.[1] A month later, President Kennedy sent a letter to the speaker of the house, John McCormack (D-MA), to propose new immigration legislation that would eliminate discrimination based on national origin.[2] Kennedy's newfound attention to inequality continued throughout the year, reaching even the local level.[3]

Yet President Kennedy did more than just act: he enlisted Congress to follow suit. As a consequence, the Eighty-Eighth Congress passed the 1964 Civil Rights Act, a piece of legislation that is rivaled only by policies introduced during the Reconstruction Era. Not to be outdone, the Supreme Court under the leadership of Earl Warren reviewed the largest number of minority-related cases in the court's history in 1964. [4]

The governmental response following Birmingham poses some interesting questions for scholars of political behavior and political institutions. Most notably, do protest actions truly influence the behavior of political officials? The timing of the events in Birmingham and the federal government's response clearly suggest they do. But when events such as these seem to influence political institutions, is it merely a coincidence, or can a link between political protest and the actions of the federal government be demonstrated?

This book attempts to address these questions by picking up from where protest ends; it sits at the intersection between the close of appeals for minority equality and the initiation of governmental policy. The chapters that follow show that protest has a demonstrable effect on governmental actions at the national level. The relationship between political protest

[1] "Letters to the Secretary of Defense and to the Chairman, Committee on Equal Opportunity in the Armed Forces, in Response to the Committee's Report." June 22, 1963.

[2] "Letter to the President of the Senate and to the Speaker of the House on Revision of the Immigration Laws." July 23, 1963.

[3] For example, on September 24, 1963, President Kennedy met with civic and political leaders in Birmingham to attempt to restore communications between white and black communities. (Indicated in "Statement by the President Following Meeting with Civic Leaders and Members of the Clergy of Birmingham". September 24, 1963.)

[4] United States Supreme Court Database (1955–1997).

and federal institutions is not straightforward. Racial and ethnic minority protest succeeds in obtaining policy change and directing federal attention when it informs politicians on the best course of action. The information received by politicians is fueled by the social context of protest behavior that involves both moderate and contentious tactics, a strong organizational structure, and a significant number of engagers who persist over time. These factors accumulate to signal the saliency of racial and ethnic minority concerns and draw the government's attention to political issues that are rising in importance. As pro-minority rights behavior grew in salience and the numbers of anti-minority rights actions declined, federal politicians embraced the move toward a more egalitarian society and implemented policies that would facilitate racial justice and equality. Political protest behavior thus made politicians aware of a potential area of political innovation, provided cues that demonstrated the saliency of minority concerns, and indicated which direction of political response would be best aligned with the side of protest activity most actively expressing its grievances. In brief, political officials learned from minority protest and responded when they felt emboldened by the strong informational cues provided by citizens' behavior.

Modern Perspectives on the Impact of Minority Protest

For many Americans, the 1964 Civil Rights Act and 1965 Voting Rights Act serve as lingering testaments to the impact of minority protest on policy. In fact, citizens' positive perceptions of the effectiveness of minority political protest have continued to grow over time. A 2008 Gallop Poll, for example, revealed that nearly 90 percent of Americans felt that the protesters in the civil rights movement had achieved some or all of their goals (Saad 2008). This understanding extends into a post–civil rights era in which citizens, particularly racial and ethnic minorities, view protest activities as a viable way of influencing the actions of federal politicians.

Unfortunately, there is not a substantial amount of scholarly work that evaluates this view of the efficacy of minority protest. The few scholarly works that have addressed the link between minority protest and policy reach differing conclusions. On occasion, scholars have provided evidence that citizens' protest actions are able to influence political institutions. Some argue that the mass rioting around welfare between 1964 and 1968 led to President Johnson's establishing a riot commission that "called for 'a massive and sustained commitment to action' to end poverty and racial discrimination" (Piven and Cloward 1977, 272–73). Others have taken a qualitative approach to demonstrate the influence of protest at the local level. For example, a 1989 case study of four cities in Florida demonstrates that minority protest behavior achieved marked gains with local government (Button 1989). In Mississippi, protest behavior aided the success of the War on Poverty program by increasing citizen participation, and it facilitated school desegregation in the 1970s and 1980s (Andrews 2004). A more rigorous statistical approach similarly revealed a strong positive link between minority protests and federal aid programs that benefited minority communities (Fording 1997).

For the many positive studies that demonstrate the influence of minority protest, authors have reached another set of conclusions that refute these claims. In reexamining Piven and Cloward's research (1971; 1977), Albritton (1979) finds no support for the notion that mass protest efforts produced a response from the government by increasing welfare and the size of the federal caseloads taken by the Aid to Families with Dependent Children programs during Johnson's administration. In contrast to other works that followed, Welch (1975) shows that riots in the late 1960s did not result in increased expenditures on social welfare. Adding to this chorus of opposition, some argue that civil rights demonstrations and urban riots did little to increase the president's attention to racial issues in his State of the Union addresses during the post–civil rights movement era

(Hill 1998). This side posits that political protest has an indirect effect at best, working within public opinion to influence congressional policies, as some have argued was the case for the passage of Equal Employment Opportunity legislation (Burstein 1999).[5] At worst, political protest activities have produced a negative response from government (Davenport 2010).[6]

Ironically, the line drawn in the sand by these two perspectives does not indicate that either side offers an erroneous account of protest, but rather that both are incomplete – a shared limitation that has accentuated this divide. No work, for example, offers a holistic understanding of the impact of minority protest across the three federal branches of government. The different federal branches have unique institutional constraints that limit their ability to respond to minority activity. In comparison to appointed officials, moreover, elected officials face different incentives to respond. Consider the lifelong appointments of Supreme Court justices in comparison to the relatively brief terms of elected members of Congress. Whereas the former are immune from the demands of reelection, the latter must appeal to citizens every two to six years. If we fail to juxtapose the responses of Supreme Court justices to those of members of Congress and the executive, we address only fragments of a larger story of government response to minority behavior. Consequently, our theoretical and analytical focus should be on the forest and not the trees of protest influence – focusing on the "macropolity" of government that includes an understanding of responsiveness

[5] Joseph Luders (2010) makes a similar point, arguing that politicians during the civil rights movement strongly considered the preferences of third-party bystanders in their cost calculations regarding whether to respond to protest actions. Some have also argued that even though protest may have aided the passage of the 1964 Civil Rights Act, public opinion was the dominant force that allowed the adoption of the 1972 Equal Employment Opportunity Act (Santoro 2002).

[6] Even at the local level, studies show that several city officials in California from 1960 to 1980 ignored protest activities from minority groups that were conducted without the aid of a dominant multiracial coalition and electoral mobilization (Browning, Marshall, and Tabb 1984).

across multiple institutions.[7] As we shall see in the chapters that follow, when some federal institutions turned a blind eye to the grievances expressed by protestors, others championed these concerns, becoming enthusiastic exponents of diversity and racial equality.

The divide between varying accounts of protest influence is further deepened by studies' lack of quantifiable measures that consider the social context of protest actions. Historical examinations of minority protest create a lucid story of events. These in-depth case studies address various components of minority behavior, such as a movement's organizational structure and the social conditions in which minority protest actions took place. But this rich historical perspective does not always translate well into quantitative studies of protest outcomes. As a consequence, these historical insights are only partially reflected in statistical analyses (or, worse, excluded altogether). If we fail to distinguish the context in which protest activity takes place, we risk treating all protest as monolithic, each event indistinguishable from the next. We require an interdisciplinary theory that takes into account the comprehensive way in which minority protest may exercise an influence on federal government.

Minority Protest as a Continuum of Information

My theory of governmental response is an alterative approach to conceptualizing the impact of minority political behavior that broadens both our view of protest and the framework of citizens' influence. In doing so, my revision of the current narrative shifts from considering specific attributes of political protest that may influence government to demonstrating how these various characteristics combine to offer a

[7] The term "macropolity" comes from the encompassing work of Robert Erikson, Michael Mackuen, and James Stimson (2002, 427), who successfully expands our understanding of public opinion by focusing collective attitudes across multiples institutions and across a half decade. They term this collective understanding the "macropolity," a concept that I embrace in this book.

global perspective on issues most affecting racial and ethnic minorities. There are, indeed, gradations of protest actions, and some protests give greater voice to minority concerns and allow them to resonate with governmental officials. But in order to offer a more expansive view of responsiveness, I begin this narrative of protest influence with the politicians who are viewing these actions and their motivations for recognizing minority interests alongside, and at times counter to, majoritarian preferences. To explore this collective response, I embrace a common understanding of the incentive behind minority political protest that is shared by the various politicians across the different national institutions – that is, minority protest actions are informative to politicians, and the information they contain is used to improve governance.

Democratic theory offers a basis for my understanding. If there is a place for minority voices in a democracy, it is likely subordinate to the political preferences of the majority, which convey the "will of the people." But the will of the majority, as the framers foresaw, can impede the political concerns of minority groups. James Madison acknowledged the potential perils of a strong majority in Federalist 51: "If a majority be united by a common interest, the rights of the minority will be insecure." The solution to this problem, Madison argued, was to replace direct democracy with representative government.

Within a representative government, political officials must interpret the needs of the people. Madison writes in Federalist 10 that the aim of representative government is to "refine and enlarge the public views by passing them through the medium of a chosen body of citizens, whose wisdom may best discern the true interest of their country and whose patriotism and love of justice will be least likely to sacrifice it to temporary or partial considerations." In this passage, Madison contends that the role of political representatives is to distinguish between what citizens want and that which is best for the nation. This is an indispensable role of political representatives because it allows government, or, rather, the people who lead, to stand against majority preference when minority concerns reflect a more just path.

But how are political officials informed of minority concerns? Even in a representative government, elected officials require cues that will indicate the political preferences of racial and ethnic minorities. Political protest has often served as this cue, and the social context in which protests occur provides signals to politicians about the scope of citizens' activism. By "scope," I refer to the unique attributes of political protest that distinguish one form of citizen behavior from another. A strike involving fifteen random disgruntled employees protesting discriminatory employment practices, for instance, is likely to be perceived differently by politicians than a protest event that is backed by a political organization, involves ten thousand minority citizens marching on a state capital over several days, and ends with a number of arrests or even an unfortunate death. The difference between these two events is the *scope* of the protest actions: the former is small, unorganized, and peaceful, whereas the latter is fairly large, well-organized, and contentious. The scope of protest goes beyond the internal characteristics of political activism, moreover, to include competing protests that advocate the opposing position on a political topic and vie for the attention of government. The social environment that is created and shaped by the scope of political actions has characteristics that also shape political opportunities.

At the most basic level, minority protest informs every branch of government of the importance of racial and ethnic minority concerns, which allows for political innovation. This not only inspires politicians to address new issues but also allows political officials to adapt to the constant evolution of minority appeals. Furthermore, evaluating the context of minority protest allows politicians to prioritize racial and ethnic concerns and rank-order these issues in comparison to the other problems facing the nation. Finally, the competing protest activities conducted on race also guide the government's response: as one side of protest actions cedes issue space to another, this directs the course of action a politician should take.[8]

My theoretical approach shifts the focus away from unique, individual characteristics of minority protest to a perspective that combines the multiple facets of political behavior to offer a more complete understanding of citizens' action. More specifically, I reconceive minority protest as a *continuum of information* that indicates the importance of addressing race. This conception casts politicians in a different light: they are not always forced to the bargaining table by extremist activists or held hostage by an uncontrollable crisis situation. Politicians are also strategic collectors of information who offer a response once they have been persuaded that addressing issues of race is in the best interest of the American people.

Defining Governmental Response to a Collective Minority

If government indeed responds to minority political behavior, how can we recognize that response? My interest lies strictly in defining what constitutes a federal governmental response.[9] I do not want to define this response simply in terms of public policies but rather to try to tap into various stages of the entire policy-making process for each federal institution, which can also include the *potential* for governmental action. Thus, I focus on the rhetoric of politicians, their political decisions, their nonpolicy actions, and the policy results, both for collective institutions and for individual representatives and justices.

[8] The idea that protest can be informative to politicians has also been seen in the work of Susanne Lohmann (1993), who posits that cues from protest activity has the potential to make "socially invisible" issues politically salient (329). In this light, the collective actions of citizens become a form of communication for politicians (Mansbridge 1994). The work of King and Soule (2007) also express protest as being informative events that influence the stock prices of corporations.

[9] My reason for doing so is that the federal response has not been given adequate treatment. It also presents the most controversy for scholars, which makes it a problem worth solving.

I also consider carefully who to include among those "minority" groups shaping the federal governmental response. To successfully explore the effects of minority political protest on governmental responsiveness, we must expand the scholarly focus beyond African American engagement. The black/white dichotomy has been a fixture for discussions of race, but it offers an incomplete story of minority appeals for equality. African Americans, Latinos, and Asian Americans have all contributed to highlighting issues that have troubled the minority community.

African Americans led the way with the civil rights movement. Sparked by the 1954 *Brown vs. Board of Education* decision, the black community was moved to go beyond the ballot box and employ other political tools. Ranging from the nonviolent approaches of Reverend Dr. Martin Luther King Jr. to the more aggressive tactics of Huey Newton and Bobby Steele, blacks voiced their discontent with class differences, economic woes, and social injustices. These issues touched a core within the black community, mobilizing widespread political engagement.

The organizational structure and political tactics of the civil rights movement served as a blueprint for other ethnic minority groups to voice their concerns to government. Latinos learned from this blueprint (Garcia and de la Garza 1977). Mexican Americans, the largest Latino subgroup, sprang to the political forefront with the Chicano Movement in the mid-1960s. The goals of this movement were cultural regeneration and political power. The Puerto Rican community, the second largest Latino subgroup, also experienced a heightened amount of unconventional political activity in the 1960s. In New York and elsewhere, Puerto Ricans rallied behind the Young Lords, a militant group that sought to address the inequality of Puerto Ricans on the island and in U.S. mainland ghettos.

Asian Americans also embraced protest actions in the late 1960s and early 1970s, establishing a movement that began with the San Francisco strike in 1968. The beginning stages of this movement consisted of young Asian American students collectively engaging in strikes to demand open admissions, ethnic studies, and a redefinition of the education system. The movement expanded from this base to incorporate the elderly, workers, former prison inmates, and high-school youth (Omatsu 1994). Speaking of the Asian American movement of the 1960s and 1970s, Omatsu states, "They were the people who demonstrated at eviction sites, packed City Hall hearing rooms, volunteered to staff health fairs.... They were the women and men who took the concept of 'serve the people' and turned it into a material force, transforming the political face of our communities" (28).

This movement behavior formed the foundation of a collective minority voice that continued to speak in the 1980s and 1990s, when protest over police brutality, immigration reform, and voter irregularities galvanized black, Latino, and Asian American communities alike. Over time, a racial and ethnic minority coalition has formed. These distinct groups have become linked through their similar appeals to national institutions for fairness and equality.

Contribution and Implications

This book is not simply about the lives and actions of racial and ethnic minorities, though the impressive historical scale of minority protest in the United States provides a wealth of knowledge with which to consider the influence of protest activism. Rather, the parallel subject of this study moves beyond the actions of marginalized groups to confront a larger and more challenging theme: viewing political protest as a form of democratic expression, and therefore a component of democratic responsiveness. Generally conceived, democratic responsiveness is the relationship between the government and the citizens whom it governs, where politicians' decisions are guided by the preferences of citizens. We have come to understand citizens' preferences as majoritarian attitudes that can be gleaned from public opinion or electoral outcomes, largely because these express mass preferences, or the general consensus of Americans across a broad range of issues. Political protest, however, is often eschewed from this conventional picture of responsiveness in favor of other forms of mass sentiment.

In my view, this omission creates a limited conception of responsiveness that constrains the eclectic mix of the nation's views to institutionalized behavior and structured polling. Citizens' preferences are not monolithic or consistent across issues; at times, a single issue inspires gradients of sentiment, from passionate discontent to complete acceptance. More to the point, citizens are sometimes moved by events and tragedies in ways that cannot be measured by the passivity of public opinion polls or delayed for an election cycle. In such events, people are compelled to act, and political protest is the avenue through which they can express their most urgent concerns. In doing so, their protest behavior becomes another vehicle by which they communicate to government.[10]

This book, therefore, offers a refinement of democratic responsiveness theory and contributes to our understanding of the policy results that follow from non-electoral behavior, specifically, protest actions. The body of scholarly work produced by both sociologists and political scientists has paid little attention to the link between political protest and government responsiveness.[11] The lack of attention to this topic is understandable, if unexpected. Sociological studies tend to be interested in what motivates individuals to participate in

[10] The information provided by political protest can also initiate a national dialogue on inequality for marginalized groups in deliberative democracy – a form of government where citizens and politicians engage in public discourse over policies. Amy Gutmann and Dennis Thompson (2004) state, "Some issues cannot even reach the political agenda unless some citizens are willing to act with passion, making statements and declarations rather than developing arguments and responses. When non-deliberative politics, antiwar marches, sit-ins, and workers' strikes are necessary to achieve deliberative ends…these actions often provoke more deliberation than would otherwise occur" (51).

[11] Doug McAdam and Sidney Tarrow (2010), two leading scholars of sociology, offered a similar critique of both fields.

movements, how movements are formed and sustained, and how movement behavior affects societal conditions. This research, until recently, rarely addressed political institutions and the factors that influence political actors.[12] Whereas political scientists are more accustomed to recognize the factors that influence political institutions, on the other hand, they have struggled to offer much insight into the political outcomes of protest behavior.[13] As opposed to understanding citizens' preferences through non-electoral political behavior or political protest, the discussion in political science has revolved around the factors that determine citizens' engagement in political behavior, with a strong emphasis on voting activity.[14] Consequently, political science research has been slow to recognize the connection that Sidney Verba and Norman Nie pushed for nearly forty years ago: "Responsiveness is what democracy is supposed to be about and, more specifically, is what participation is supposed to increase" (1972, 300).[15]

[12] There are several exceptions, as well as a newfound surge of research that is starting to examine the consequences of movement behavior in sociology. For example, see McAdam and Su 2002; Amenta 2006; Amenta and Caren 2004; Agnone 2007; Andrews 2004; Giugni 2004; 2007; Kane 2003; King et al. 2005; King et al. 2007; McCammon et al. 2001; Soule and Olzak 2004; Olzak and Soule 2009; Soule and King 2006; Soule and Davenport 2009; and Luders 2010. This is only a cursory list of the burgeoning new research being produced. For an excellent review of works that link protest to governmental outcomes, see Amenta, Caren, Chiarello, and Su 2010.

[13] There are notable exceptions to this trend (e.g., Baumgartner and Mahoney 2005; Browning, Marshall, and Tabb 1986; Fording 1997; Campbell 2003; Parker 2009; Piven and Cloward 1977; Verba and Nie 1972). Andrea Campbell's (2003) discussion of senior political activism and the welfare state impressively explores not only the impact that citizens have on government but also the ability of government to influence citizens' behavior.

[14] In comparing the two disciplines of political science and sociology, even the terminology is different. Here and throughout the book, I refer to the non-electoral behavior I investigate as "political protest," for these are protest actions that seek to influence the political system. However, these same actions are classified as "movement behavior" by sociologists. In essence, the two fields have addressed the same political phenomenon, citizens' behavior, but in two separate spheres. The terminology gap may have contributed to the lack of interdisciplinary work on the topic.

[15] The words of Sidney Verba and Norman Nie also force us to reflect on the limited ways in which we view and study political participation. Political

This book embraces this notion and establishes a direct link between protest behavior and political institutions.

Given the influence that minority protest actions have wielded over national government, the implication drawn from this approach to understanding protest is a powerful one. Minorities' shift from protest to politics as a political strategy has opened the door for institutionalized political opportunity. Yet it has also inadvertently neglected a successful avenue for racial and ethnic minorities to have their voices heard. Thus, in the post–civil rights era, the decline in federal governmental policies addressing race is not simply driven by previous policy successes or by the existence of fewer problems in the minority community. It is also a result of the limited number of behavioral cues that inform national institutions on the state of social and economic inequality.

Structure of the Book

In the chapters to come, I aim to answer the central question driving this study: Do racial and ethnic minority protest actions directly influence the actions of federal politicians and the policies stemming from national political institutions?

In Chapter 1, I lay out my *continuum of information theory*, providing the theoretical foundation to address this question. I argue that current conceptions of minority protest focus on one or two major characteristics of political protest, as opposed to considering the complete array of attributes that make up the entire scope of political behavior. Once the unique characteristics of protest are combined and placed on a continuum, it is possible to see how political behavior provides informative cues to politicians that indicate the saliency of racial and ethnic minority concerns. I also detail how different national institutions use this information to govern.

participation is an array of different modes of activity. Though some forms of participation, such as protest, lack an institutionalized procedure to implement the concerns voiced therein, these actions still have meaning for politicians.

Chapter 2 examines variation in racial and ethnic minority political protest over time and by geographical location. This chapter begins by discussing the previous definitions and measures of minority protest and examines how these earlier assessments capture only pieces of protests' influence. The chapter goes on to present a more encompassing approach that accounts for the multiple characteristics of political behavior that combine to indicate the importance of racial and ethnic minority concerns. Using this reconception of political behavior and newspaper accounts of political protest drawn from the Dynamics of Collective Action dataset, I examine the geographical location of minority protest at the U.S. county level over four decades: the 1960s, 1970s, 1980s, and 1990s. This chapter shows that the scope of minority protest not only fluctuated over time but also spread across the nation as we moved to a post–civil rights era. The diffusion of political protest heightened the public's attention to race and cemented minority concerns as some of the most critical problems facing the nation. By considering temporal and geographic variations in minority protest alongside public perceptions of the saliency of minority concerns, I am able to specify the palpable political climate created by minority political behavior at various points over the period of study.

Chapters 3–5 seek to link the information in minority protest to a governmental response from three federal branches of government. In Chapter 3, I begin by examining the collective body of Congress. I explore whether the information in minority protest was able to dictate the number of congressional hearings and laws enacted that involved racial and ethnic minority concerns. After discussing the impact of minority protest at the aggregate level, the second section of this chapter shifts the focus to how individual representatives respond to minority appeals. Here, I highlight legislators' individual voting records, which are derived from ideal point scores of liberalism as well as Leadership Conference on Civil Rights (LCCR) scores, and I link these votes to racial and ethnic minority protest originating from their districts, as opposed to protest occurring elsewhere. This chapter demonstrates that national minority protest behavior is not able to change aggregate decisions made by Congress. The relationship is more nuanced than that. To understand minority concerns voiced through political behavior, congressional leaders, figuratively speaking, turn to their backyards. Politicians look at the content of minority protest actions that lie within their own districts and react to the non-electoral political behavior of their constituents.

In Chapter 4, I continue this analysis of the federal response with an examination of the president's actions and rhetoric. Using an original dataset drawn from information in the *Federal Register* and volumes of the *Public Papers of the Presidents* series, I examine the content of presidential letters, press conferences, public statements, memoranda, executive orders, and State of the Union addresses. Considering every president from Dwight Eisenhower to William Clinton, I illustrate the influence that informative protest actions had on each mode of presidential action and show how this influence moved between private responses and those in a public forum. This chapter illustrates that presidents were responsive to salient forms of minority protest, and this response was often favorable. Moreover, presidents elected by either political party were responsive to issues of race. Even though the majority of their reactions came in the form of rhetoric as opposed to executive policies, presidents acted swiftly.

I complete the analysis of governmental responsiveness in Chapter 5 with an examination of Supreme Court cases and rulings. This chapter discusses both the Supreme Court's rulings and the selection of racial and ethnic minority cases under the Warren, Burger, and Rehnquist Courts in response to political protest. It explores the question of whether life-tenure appointments and norms of ruling based on precedent are, at times, overshadowed by the external influence of minority political protest. After separating the U.S. Supreme Court database (Speath 1999) into various policy issues that relate to race, I conduct statistical analysis on justices' aggregate and individual rulings. This chapter reveals that individual justices do indeed become attentive to informative protest once citizens' actions stimulate national public opinion on race relations. Unlike the influence on other institutions, political protest first changes public perceptions and later works within a heightened environment of public opinion to influence liberal and conservative justices' decisions. Liberal justices, in particular, are receptive to information stemming from political protest. While extremely liberal justices like Marshall or Brennan were likely to be favorable toward minority issues, they were further emboldened to act by societal conditions that supported racial and ethnic minority concerns.

I conclude by discussing the major contributions of my theory and the value of empirically considering a national response across the three branches of government. Finally, I explain the implications of my findings for the contemporary period. I argue that racial and ethnic minorities' shift away from political protest over the last fifty years has left politicians less informed on the policies affecting minority communities. With less information stemming from minority protest to help shape and promote federal policies, racial progress has considerably slowed in this nation.

I

A Continuum of Information

The Influence of Minority Political Protest

But if, even in America, with its universal creed of democracy and equality, there are great inequalities in the conditions of different citizens, must there not also be great inequalities in the capacities of different citizens to influence the decisions of their various governments? And if, because they are unequal in other conditions, citizens of a democracy are unequal in power to control their government, then who in fact does govern?

– *Robert Dahl*

Both tears and sweat are salty, but they render a different result. Tears will get you sympathy; sweat will get you change.

– *Jesse Jackson*

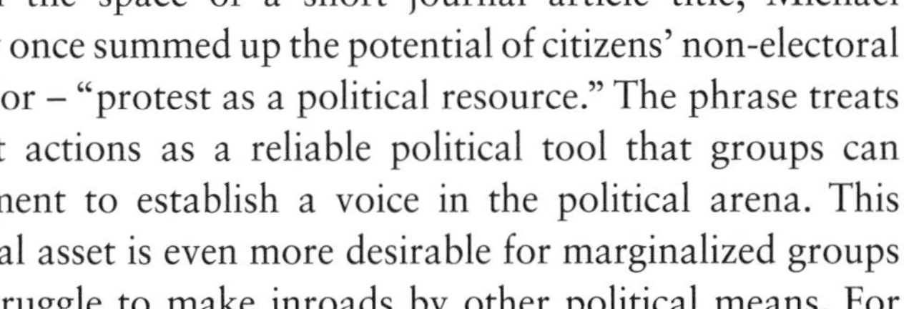

Within the space of a short journal article title, Michael Lipsky once summed up the potential of citizens' non-electoral behavior – "protest as a political resource." The phrase treats protest actions as a reliable political tool that groups can implement to establish a voice in the political arena. This political asset is even more desirable for marginalized groups that struggle to make inroads by other political means. For relatively powerless groups, protest actions can, to borrow Lipsky's words, "increase their bargaining ability" in the political discourse. In this conception, protest actions are inherent to the political process. No institutionalized procedure exists, however, to translate the concerns voiced in political protest into governmental policies. In addition, protest actions lack an enforcing mechanism that mandates a response from governmental officials. Yet even in the absence of an institutional link, minority protest actions may resonate with politicians.

This chapter delves into the causal mechanisms by which minority protest informs politicians. I move momentarily beyond this volume's focus on minority concerns to fit my theoretical claims into a larger discussion of governmental response and political protest. What emerges is a holistic theory that views minority protest as consisting of moving parts that combine to offer signals to politicians regarding the importance of addressing race-related issues. This theory, referred to as a "continuum of information," offers a framework that explains which characteristics of minority protest are informative to politicians, indicates how these distinct attributes coalesce to signal the saliency of a given protest issue, and explains how these cues compete with signals on the opposite side of the issue space. Finally, and perhaps most important, I describe why national political actors in each of the three branches of government are attuned to political protest and how this attention translates into a governmental response.

Focusing on the Parts in the Sum of Protest

Scholars have long sought to understand the dynamic process that connects political behavior to governmental outcomes (McAdam et al. 2001), producing rich theories that help to clarify the link between political activism and policy success. An inadvertent byproduct of these detailed theories is a body of literature that seeks to pinpoint which specific characteristics of protest behavior facilitate change. Scholars have identified four broad attributes of protest that influence government: levels of contention, organizational structure, signals of ideological preference, and political framing.

The level of contention has received probably the greatest attention of these four attributes. While I refer to it here as "contention," it has been called "disruption," "crisis," "violence," and "instability." Powerless groups rely on contention to influence the political arena. Contentious political protest disrupts the public order and produces negative inducements for political elites to engage in bargaining (Lipsky 1968). Frances Piven and Richard Cloward argue that the contentious aspect of political protest is key to understanding its success in influencing policy. "The most useful way to think about the effectiveness of protest," they argue, "is to examine the disruptive tactics" (1977, 24). The "political reverberations" of disruption are an important political tool for racial and ethnic minorities. The disruptive tactics employed in the civil rights movement, in particular, succeeded in pushing Democrats closer to a party platform more favorable to minorities by "exacerbating electoral instabilities which had already been set in motion by economic moderation in the South" (183).

Contentious behavior can also be implemented as a deliberate tactical approach to increase a group's bargaining power (McAdam 1983). Though known for his nonviolent tactics, Martin Luther King Jr. was aware of the leverage that accompanied a contentious political environment. In referring to the events of Birmingham, King claimed that the key to everything was federal commitment. To secure this, he expounded, you had to "set out to precipitate a crisis situation that must open the door to negotiation" (qtd. in Garrow 1999, 228). Empirical studies support this claim. In comparison to passive or moderate political behavior, "unruly groups" that employ "violence, strikes, and other constraints" are more likely to succeed (Gamson 1975, 87). A number of studies associate disruption with governmental policy change (e.g., McAdam and Su 2002; Fording 1997).

The organizational structure of political behavior also influences its effectiveness. A sustained organizational infrastructure provides movement behavior with strong leadership, informal political ties, and financial resources from an established membership base (Andrews 2004, 25). An organization's ability to implement programs, challenge political authority, and employ tactics that persuade government to act relies on this structure (Andrews 2001, 90). Political organizations are also important because they are the mechanism that conveys protesters' interests to politicians. Daniel Cress and David Snow argue that "viable organizations" with the ability to "accumulate resources and engage in elaborated and focused framing discussions" are necessary for political behavior to create the sort of sustainable challenge government acts upon (2000, 1100).

Yet another factor that affects the outcome of protest is the political preferences of citizens engaged in this political behavior. As studies of lobbying make clear (Spence 1973), governmental officials are more likely to favor citizen actions that express concerns in concert with the officials' own ideological beliefs (Banks 1999). Susanne Lohmann explores citizen preferences in protest activities through a signaling model that accounts for the size of mass political action. The size of political protest offers politicians an indication of where majoritarian values lie. Lohmann argues that an "office-motivated leader might be more likely to remain in power if the leader's policy decisions benefit a majority" (1993, 320). The number of participants in mass political protest must pass a threshold, however, before the protest can effectively signal a majority preference for policy change. While larger protests are likely to prompt greater responsiveness, Lohmann believes that governmental officials will discount more contentious political behavior, which reflects the involvement of extreme political activists who lie farther from the median voter and thus from the policy preferences of the majority. In this perspective, one characteristic of political protest (contention) directly contradicts another (size).

A final aspect of minority protests that leads to policy success is the framing of an issue (Babb 1996; Tarrow 1992; Gamson 1992; Snow and Benford 1988). Protest participants who frame their issue around a popular belief can expand their support to the general public (McCammon 1995; Quadagno 1992). Protest participants can also benefit from having a narrowly tailored message that identifies the problem, recognizes the culpable parties, and proposes policies that alleviate concerns (Cress and Snow 2000; Snow and Benford 1988). Thus, it is important to consider not only protesters' actions but also the message they convey.

All four conceptions of protest point to important characteristics of political behavior. Yet they draw our attention to one or two influential attributes of protest actions. In practice, however, it is difficult to imagine that politicians would recognize the size of a political event but ignore the contentious nature of citizens' actions, or examine the disruptive tactics used in an event but disregard the social and political organizations that support it. Cress and Snow (2000) make a keen point in this regard, arguing that conceptions of protest that focus "on the ways in which different conditions interact and combine are likely to be more compelling and robust, both theoretically and empirically, than efforts that focus on the conditions specified by a single perspective or that pit one perspective against another." I concur with this assertion and wish to expand upon it. The social characteristics highlighted in previous theoretical claims are but a few pieces of the larger informational context. In fact, the entirety of minority protest offers politicians a rich understanding of political activism and contributes to what I refer to as the continuum of information.

The Continuum of Information Theory

The continuum of information theory posits that the unique characteristics of minority political protest provide valuable cues to political officials regarding concerns present in racial and ethnic minority communities. These cues, in turn, engender greater information that afford politicians opportunities to take confident action. The central claim of the theory

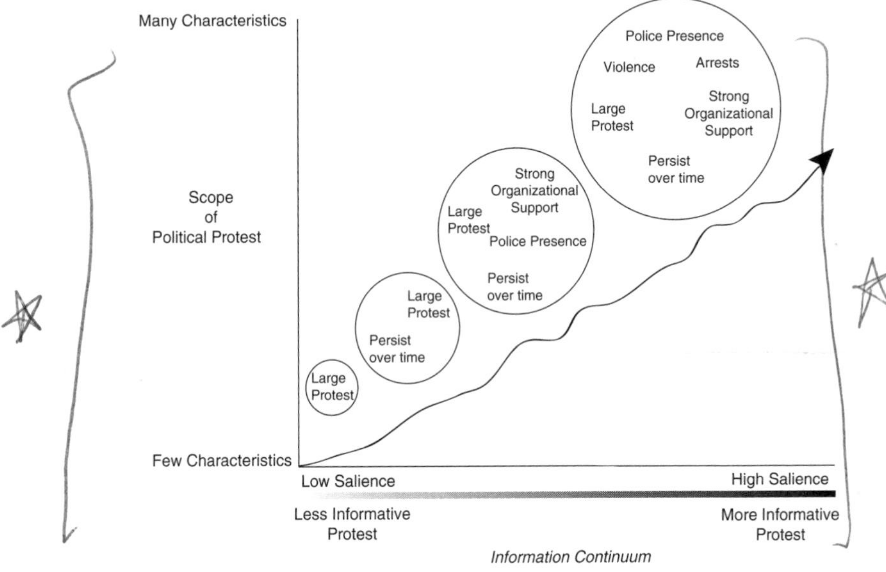

FIGURE 1.1. Information continuum.

is that the *scope* of minority protest, driven by the social characteristics of political activism, influences the attention of government and the direction of governmental action. The scope of minority protest also provides informative signals that politicians use to vary their responses. Multiple features of non-electoral behavior that indicate the strength of political protest combine to offer politicians a holistic understanding of citizens' concerns.

No government official can be informed about every political topic. They rely upon the changing political and social environment to update their understanding of issues, and potentially their beliefs (Ferejohn and Kuklinski 1990). The information provided by minority protest serves as an avenue that governmental officials can use to better understand race-related issues. The information they gather from citizens' behavior updates uninformed politicians' understanding of the state of the world (Lohmann 1993).

In Figure 1.1, I highlight the attributes of political protest that can be placed on an information continuum. In this diagram, the vertical axis depicts, in no particular order, the characteristics of protest that become known to politicians.[1] As the various characteristics of minority protest are revealed, this new information affects politicians' overall perception of the protest behavior and increases the issue's level of salience along the horizontal axis, thus expanding the scope of political protest.

The size and durability of protest, as well as protesters' organizational structure, shape the saliency of political events.  Inherent in political protest is the need to overcome the collective action problem, which is the reluctance of individuals to forego the pursuit of their personal objectives in favor of group goals (Chong 1991). As protests grow larger, they demonstrate that a greater number of individuals are willing to relinquish their unique grievances to pursue a more general aim, demonstrating their commitment to the political cause in question. The persistence of this commitment can be gleaned from the duration of minority protests.[2] Short-lived political action reflects the momentary importance of political issues, whereas a constant appeal to government indicates that the citizens involved are dedicated to political change. Hence, the size and duration of protest events offer valuable information. The Montgomery Bus Boycott is illustrative of both these points. Blacks in Montgomery coordinated their efforts in massive numbers to collectively oppose the city bus system. This commitment was then reinforced over the 381 days that boycotters endured cramped car rides or miles of walking to the workplace to forgo public transportation.

[1] While politicians may assign greater weight to specific social characteristics in protest activity, there is likely to be a lack of consensus regarding which attributes are most salient. Thus, I conceptualize the unique components of political protest as being equally important. This approach allows for a more general analysis.

[2] Both the size of protest and the commitment protestors have for their issues are also components found in Charles Tilly's WUNC acronym. This acronym refers to worthiness, unity, numbers, and commitment. The numbers and commitment seen in protest are displays that garner attention from local observers (Tilly 2006, 53–54).

The organizational structure of minority protest is also informative to political leaders, enhancing activists' credibility. Organizations invest their financial resources, membership, and knowledge to back political action. When the National Association for the Advancement of Colored Peoples, Urban League, American Civil Liberties Union, or La Raza is connected to a political protest, they provide greater legitimacy to the claims expressed in these events.

More contentious aspects of political protest can be equally important in shaping their salience. Protest actions that involve property damage, arrests, violence, injury, and even death convey the ardor that citizens feel toward an issue. Whether contention is instigated by participants or withstood by activists, government becomes cognizant that institutionalized modes of political engagement, namely, voting, have failed to capture the passion that citizens feel about a particular issue or the severity of a problem.

These multiple characteristics of political protest work in conjunction with one another to inform political officials. However, the information that politicians gather from political protest does not stem from one side only. Opposing voices compete in the political arena to express their concerns. In protest activity, movement–countermovement behavior reveals these voices. With regard to minority concerns, the progressive rulings of the courts in the mid-1950s and the political behavior of minority organizations resulted in severe backlash. This was most evident in the implementation of school integration, which aroused fears and anger in some white Americans who were unwilling to change the status quo. This backlash continued into the early 1960s, when anti-minority protests were common. White supremacist organizations mobilized and responded to black political behavior (McAdam 1982, 172–73). In many instances, the opposing sides faced off in the streets to express their views.

Yet the clash between opposing sides does more than inform politicians of opposing views: it is also a competition for issue ownership. As David Meyer and Suzanne Staggenborg explain,

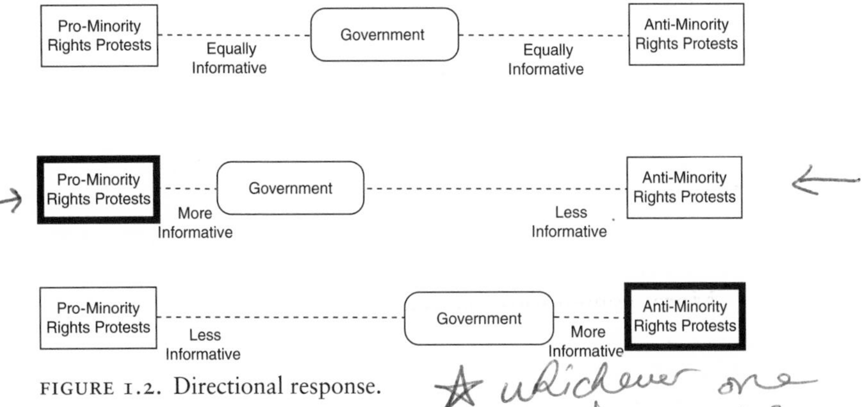

FIGURE 1.2. Directional response.

the two sides "make competing claims on the state on matters of policy and politics ... and vie for attention from the mass media and the broader public" (1996, 1632). The claims both sides make feed into public perceptions and direct the government's response. The competing voices also indicate the congruity of appeals expressed in political protest. Figure 1.2 illustrates the tug-of-war that exists between opposing views.

At times, citizens engage in mass protest actions that are extremely informative, and still government does not respond. The tug-of-war between sides also serves to explain these periods of inactivity. When the context of protest actions stemming from one side of activism is matched by equally salient forms of political behavior originating from countermovements, political officials face a dilemma. In this situation, protest action loses its ability to direct government, as the first image in Figure 1.2 demonstrates. Yes, the content of these political protest events is salient, and to onlookers it appears that the contentious environment would galvanize governmental attention and elicit a response. Yet the competing voices suggest to government officials that both sides have an important claim. Thus, remaining inactive or promoting the status quo will not leave a politician worse off.

The first of the three images in Figure 1.2 depicts the expectation of governmental inaction when competing sides engage in political activity that is equally informative. The next two images depict how the balance tips when more information is revealed by one side than by the other. The scope of political protest drives governmental policies to favor the most informative and salient political behaviors.

Political protest presents opportunities for politicians to engage in political innovation. Thus, citizens who engage in political protest are "policy entrepreneurs" (Polsby 1984, 167). Through their political actions, they attempt to set the political agenda and to focus governmental attention on a grievance that requires redress. The very existence of political protest leads politicians to view an issue as controversial, and the controversy signals a problem to government and the public at large (Rochon 1998, 179). But the strength of the signal varies according to the scope of protest actions. Political protest does not simply introduce political dialogue: it also alters and expands the discussion. Once political issues are brought to the attention of politicians, the relative salience of minority protest gives governmental officials a way to measure the importance of racial and ethnic minority concerns alongside other issues. In other words, politicians use the information derived from protest to rank-order the different issues on their policy agendas.

Finally, competing protest forces offer a signal to government on the best political course of action to take. The signal is not always clear, however. When the volume of pro-minority protests is matched by an equal number of anti-minority protests, the competing concerns offer mixed messages to politicians. The appeals coming from both sides wash each other out like random noise. Conversely, when pro-minority protest begins to dominate the political arena, political officials may infer the side that is still standing is the more resilient, or perhaps that the decreasing number of countermovement protests reflects the changing perspectives of the activists who initially opposed minority rights. At the very least, the decreasing number of protests by one side cedes part of its issue ownership to the other side and directs the policies issued by government.

Within this conception, political protest gives politicians the information they need to seek out and adapt to a new issue, gauge the importance of political topics, and determine the direction of their response, all of which allow politicians to improve governance.

How Political Institutions Use the Information in Political Protest

The theoretical claims expressed here rely on a simple but important assumption: that politicians are seekers of information. For each branch of government, there are institutional norms that facilitate the gathering of this information. The president is informed about international and domestic events through the President's Daily Brief. Congress holds hearings to observe the current state of affairs on a topic. And the Supreme Court reviews amicus curiae briefs to learn about critical perspectives given by both sides of a case. All are doing the same thing: attempting to become more informed about the myriad issues on which they will later have to make federal decisions. The information provided by political protests serves as a shortcut that helps politicians make decisions.

After minority protest has offered informative cues to government, political officials within each institution must still decide how to use this information. I contend that politicians are attuned to and influenced by citizens' behavior. But why should every branch of government – or any branch, for that matter – respond to citizens' minority protest activities? The answer lies in how government sets and maneuvers issues of race on the policy agenda. There is a commonality across the various branches of government that should promote a response. This commonality is that officials use minority protest as an informational cue to direct and navigate responses to salient issues; their use manifests itself differently, however, according to the unique institutional constraints on each branch of government.

Congress

For congressional scholars who examine politicians' attention to minority policies, the study of political protest and the signals that lie within is secondary to the study of individual and district-level attributes. The main focus of scholarly attention has concentrated on the importance of a representative's racial background to understand whether or not he or she actively pursues minority policies. This debate, which tends to take on new life during periods of reapportionment, is divided into two sides. One side argues that representatives' race is a driving force behind their decision to address minority interests (Canon 1999; Whitby 2002; Baker and Cook 2005). The other side views congressional leaders as being attentive to their constituents irrespective of the representative's racial background. Moreover, this side views the creation of majority-minority districts to increase minority representation in Congress as potentially undermining the passage of substantive racial policies (Cameron et al. 1996; Swain 1993). From this discussion emerges the less controversial conclusion that the racial composition of a representative's district affects his or her decisions on whether to support minority policies (Combs et al. 1984; Hutchings et al. 2004; Fleisher 1993; Lublin 1997; Overby and Cosgrove 1996). What has been largely absent from this discussion is any consideration of public sentiment within a representative's district. Of course, measuring the size of the minority population serves as a proxy for citizens' preferences. It is difficult, however, to gauge constituents' attitudes toward minority issues by observing the racial make-up of the citizen population. Political protest actions offer a clearer indication of citizens' preferences.

Political protest can alert politicians of a changing tide or of an issue that is rising in importance. Legislators are forward-looking, concerned about future issues that could potentially endanger their seats (Arnold 1990). Thus, they consider "potential preferences" that citizens may value in the future (Sulkin 2005). When legislators are not attentive to the saliency of minority protest, moreover, this provides fertile ground for challenger candidates to underscore the sitting politician's failure to address constituent concerns (Sulkin 2005).[3] Hence, politicians who ignore concerns voiced in district-level protest become vulnerable to political scrutiny.

The directional component of political protest is also important for legislators, improving the information they receive from political behavior. As we have seen, political protest is a form of lobbying for congressional leaders' votes. Citizens on both sides of an issue attempt to change legislators' predisposition with regard to minority concerns. The presence of competition encourages them to produce accurate information for politicians, since opposing groups do not want to be discredited for misrepresenting the facts (Austen-Smith and Wright 1994).

The President

The president is constantly looking to set the agenda, and his ability to do so is unmatched by that of any other single political actor (Baumgartner and Jones 1993, 241). In order for the president to set the agenda, he must identify those issues that deserve national attention. Minority political protest allows the president to recognize the importance of minority issues, and its informal cues build on the president's existing knowledge of the state of affairs. Theodore Sorensen explains, "To make informed decisions, the President must be at home with a staggering range of information.... He must cope with issues for which no previous experience on earth can equip him. For the essence of decision is choice; and, to choose, it is first necessary to know" (2005, 39). Salient political protest behavior provides the president with additional information to evaluate a given issue.

Minority protest also aids the president in prioritizing the multiple issues always on his agenda. As minority protest moves along the continuum and becomes more salient, it emerges in

[3] Sulkin (2005) makes the point that "challengers may even be able to create the perception of weakness on issues by highlighting them in their campaigns."

public perception as a relevant topic that requires attention, and it becomes more likely to receive this attention from presidents and staffers. The political protest events in Birmingham, for example, "not only affected the issue and the alternative but drove civil rights to the Kennedy must list" (Light 1982).

Downplaying or blatantly ignoring essential issues highlighted by minority protest endangers a president's reelection prospects, public approval ratings, and legacy. For those presidents who are in their first term in office, ignoring protest activities that convey the most pressing problems of the nation threatens to have a negative impact on voter support. Even after a president moves to the second term in office and becomes a lame duck, the reelection goals of members in his political party take center stage. Often, senators, members of the House of Representatives, and governors are punished when a president ignores the most important concerns on the public agenda (Piereson 1975; Gronke et al. 2003).

A president's failure to address the public's most pressing problems also encourages citizens to view the president as an individual who understands the needs of the nation but does not know how to address those concerns. This suggestion of the president's lack of competence may prompt public confidence to deteriorate. Once public confidence begins to wane, it becomes harder for the president to gather support for his legislative initiatives in Congress (Kernell 1993). Consequently, a president's decision to ignore salient minority concerns may have a ripple effect and diminish the public's willingness to support his other policies.

Supreme Court

To address the Supreme Court's response to political protest, we are forced to characterize justices in one of two lights: either as allowing societal conditions to affect their judicial decisions (Flemming 1997; Link 1995; Mishler 1993, 1996; Stimson 1995) or as ignoring public concerns (Segal 1993, 2002; Hagle and Spaeth 1993). Scholars operating with the former understanding characterize the Court as being influenced by popular sentiment and behavior. Justices are everyday individuals who are continually shaped by their life experiences, even after being seated on the Supreme Court. In the latter view, by contrast, the Court is understood to make decisions based upon precedent, the facts of the cases, or justices' individual ideological preferences; moreover, the life-long tenure of justices shields them from the demands of the voting populace. Recent literature suggests that the first conception of the Court has gained significant ground.

Yet even in the absence of a scholarly consensus, determining whether Supreme Court justices are attuned to citizens' concerns does not have to be an act of conjecture. Justices have attested to this influence. An often-cited quote comes from former Chief Justice Rehnquist (1986):

> The judges of any court of last resort, such as the Supreme Court of the United States, work in an insulated atmosphere in their courthouse where they sit on the bench hearing oral arguments or sit in their chambers writing opinions. But these same judges go home at night and read the newspapers or watch the evening news on television; they talk to their family and friends about current events. Somewhere 'out there' beyond the walls of the courthouse run currents and tides of public opinion which lap at the courthouse door.... If these tides of public opinion are sufficiently great and sufficiently sustained, they will very likely have an effect upon the decision of some of the cases decided within the courthouse. (768)

Justice Rehnquist presents a very human side to Supreme Court justices, acknowledging that they allow their moral consciences to play a role in their decision making. As Rehnquist suggests, justices' concerns about societal conditions become relevant because justices are people, with a personal, nonprofessional stake in the outcome of the cases they hear. When cases arrive before the Supreme Court that are salient and important, it becomes incumbent on justices to evaluate these societal conditions.

Similar to the executive and legislative branches, Supreme Court justices use the information found in the context of political protest to guide their actions and set their agendas. Minority political protest indicates the significance of an issue, and when political behavior moves along the continuum, the Court focuses on cases that embody the socially relevant topics expressed in protest actions. Justice Brennan (1973) states, "The Court's calendar mirrors the ever changing concerns of this society with ever more powerful and smothering government. The calendar is therefore the indispensable source for keeping the Court abreast of these concerns" (869). Citizens' political actions allow issues to gain space on the Court's calendar and signal the state of racial and ethnic minority appeals.

Expectations for the Impact of Minority Political Protest

All three branches of government have strong motivations to draw on the continuum of information political protest provides. This theory leads to several important predictions that shape our understanding of governmental response to citizens' behavior. The major expectations are as follows:

- Salient information stemming from minority protest influences congressional leaders to pass more minority-favorable laws and hold more hearings that address issues of race.
- The individual roll-call votes of representatives will also favor minority issues when the scope of pro-minority protest provides greater information about minority concerns than anti-minority behavior in congressional leaders' respective districts.
- As minority political protest provides information about racial and ethnic minority concerns, the president's rhetoric and actions will begin to reflect these concerns.
- As minority political protest provides information about minority concerns, the Supreme Court will begin to hear more minority cases and offer more minority-favorable rulings in these cases.
- The individual votes of justices will become more favorable to minority issues as the scope of pro-minority protest provides greater information about minority concerns than anti-minority behavior.

Chapters 3–5 empirically test the validity of these claims.

Considering Information Continuum Theory Alongside Political Opportunities, Repression, and Public Opinion

Information continuum theory draws on the inner workings of political protest. These are actions and strategies that lie largely within participants' control. However, these inner workings run tangential to, and at times counter to, the broader social and political context that exists outside of protest behavior (Lipsky 1970; Eisinger 1973). Many sociologists conceive of the general political context as encompassing the changing institutional structure as well as the ideological shifts of political elites. These shifts in the political environment are the foundation of the political process model (McAdam 1996, 23) and are understood to be important for understanding the capacity of protest behavior to influence governmental outcomes (Jenkins and Perrow 1977; McAdam 1982; Kitschelt 1986; Tarrow 1998; Soule and Olzak 2004).

The changing political environment also influences the type of response that government offers. Many citizens who engage in protest behavior have noble aspirations, but their actions are not always well received by government. In some cases, protest behavior relating to minority issues has led to public fear, anxiety, or discontent about the issues being voiced and the citizens who engaged in these actions. Thus, while politicians may respond with concessions and favorable policies that address the claims voiced in protest, political leaders can also take an alternative approach that represses citizens' behavior through police action. Government often adopts a repressive approach when protesters appear to threaten the lives of citizens or the legitimacy of political institutions (Earl et al. 2003; Soule and Davenport 2009). Protest conducted by racial minorities, in particular, is more likely to draw a police presence and to experience the use of repressive force by the state (Davenport et al. 2011).

The institutions of government and the individuals who represent it are the gatekeepers of social change, and these individuals' willingness to implement reform will be constrained by shifting institutional norms, procedures, and elite alliances. These institutional fluctuations do not render the information continuum inconsequential, but rather mediate its effect. The signals sent by informative minority protest, for example, will likely be easier to recognize for liberal congressional leaders who share a similar ideology to that of minority activists. In addition, the contentious nature of protest behavior may at times be viewed as seditious actions that must be repressed to maintain democratic order.

These insights from the political process model and studies of repression can provide guidance to improve the research design I employ in this study. The information in minority protest actions should be analyzed across different political institutions as well as over time to explore the influential role of the political process. Moreover, the research design should distinguish favorable governmental responses from repressive governmental reactions. This approach will accent the multiple strategies political actors may take.

Apart from the political environment, informative protest actions must also be considered in relation to mass public opinion. The continuum of information theory situates political protest as an independent factor that can directly tap into the behavior of national government – and has. This theory of influence is a major departure from other works in the movement literature that have tagged citizens' political actions as inconsequential in the absence of a mediating force, which has often been public opinion.

Giugni (2004) argues that political protest must link up with another mechanism to bring about substantive policy reform. Many have echoed this assertion. Agnone (2007), in examining environmental policy, argues for an amplification model of behavior and public opinion, while Soule and Olzak (2004) have shown the effectiveness of this interaction at the state level. Some scholars suggest that public opinion and political protest work in concert with one another to achieve policy goals (Giugni 2004; Agnone 2007; Burstein 1998; McAdam 2001; Santoro 2002). Thus, while the impact of political protest may be limited, the combination of protest and public support can enhance the potential influence that citizens' actions have on political institutions.

For racial and ethnic minority concerns, the interaction of political behavior with public opinion is understood to be especially important. Burstein's empirical work on equal employment opportunity demonstrates that public opinion is the intermediating force through which minority protest becomes relevant. He writes, "What the social protest activity of the civil rights movement did was this: it impressed upon the public the seriousness of the struggle for civil rights, and it sensitized Congress to public opinion. This was important" (1998, 90). This line of reasoning suggests minority protest does not directly influence government – a sobering conclusion. Most importantly, this conception of political protest rigorously ties minority interests to majoritarian preferences.

I argue, however, that this view potentially underestimates the direct influence of minority protest. This is not to say that minority and majoritarian preferences are not linked. I would even posit, as others have, that it is difficult to understand minority protest without considering majority public opinion. The foundation of any democratic institution is the will of the majority of citizens in that society. However, a theory that confines the impact of minority protest to heightened levels of public consensus struggles to explain government's attention to race during periods of low or even unfavorable public opinion on minority issues in which a high level of minority protest was present. The Supreme Court, for example, decided *Loving v. Virginia* in 1967, a landmark case that ended Virginia's antimiscegenation statute and consequently race-based restrictions on marriage. Although minority protest was salient in this year, favorable public opinion was not. Even five years after the decision, a Gallop poll indicated that less than 29 percent of Americans approved of interracial marriages (Schuman et al. 1998, 118).

We cannot, nevertheless, ignore the political climate that potentially shapes the reception of political behavior. Rather, we should explore how the continuum of protest information works in a favorable environment of public opinion. It very well may be the case that minority protest shapes public attitudes and therefore the public's agenda on racial issues – a possibility I investigate in the next chapter. Despite the combined effect that protest has when it links to public opinion, however, protest behavior is likely to have an independent influence on government once the context of citizens' actions is considered.

Conclusion

This chapter has laid out the theoretical foundation of the study that follows, an interdisciplinary theory that builds upon the work of scholars in political science and sociology. I consider the complete scope of minority protest and argue that minority protest can be placed on a continuum of information, wherein multiple characteristics of political behavior combine to indicate the importance of racial and ethnic minority concerns. I also posit that government has been receptive to this information. Each federal branch of government has changed its policies and behavior in response to the salience of citizens' protest actions. Before I offer the evidence to validate these claims, I will focus in the next chapter on establishing measures of salient minority protest and offering a universal methodological approach to analyzing the link between citizens and their government.

2

Measuring Information in Minority Protest

In Chapter 1, I established a theoretical foundation for understanding the direct influence of political protest. I argued that the social context of racial and ethnic minority protest was informative to the federal government and allowed politicians to be more responsive to the scope of citizens' behavior. This chapter introduces a new measure of minority protest that captures the scope of citizens' political action. It then employs this measure to consider the geographical and temporal distribution of minority protest. Not only does minority protest provide stronger informational cues in some geographical locations than others, but the strength of minority voices has fluctuated over time. Over the period of study, the cues provided by political protest have become less informative to politicians, and so has the importance of race relations. The chapter concludes with a discussion of the influence of protest events on national public perceptions of race.

Existing Approaches to Measuring Minority Protest

There are several ways to define what constitutes a minority protest event and even more ways to measure these varying definitions. The most direct approach is to examine only whether or not a collective political event occurred. This measure is straightforward and has often been used to assess movement and individual behavior around protest activities. Simply asking whether a protest event occurred, however, ignores the contextual factors that shaped the impact of citizens' behavior on government response.

Another way of measuring protest is to consider the disruption protest activities generate. The threat of social disorder can inspire reform through middle-class calculations of social cost and political elites' fear of mass violence (Lipsky 1970, 35). William Gamson (1975) is one of the most notable scholars to have measured political protest in terms of its violence. Since Gamson's intervention, scholarship on political contention has evolved to consider other aspects of protest events. Doug McAdam and Yang Su's work on threat and persuasion, for example, builds on the disruptive view of political behavior. The authors employ multiple measures that include the size of protest events, the use of violent tactics by demonstrators or law enforcement officers, property damage, and injuries to protesters (2002, 701). This approach improves upon earlier attempts to capture the context of political protest.

One potential drawback to considering disruption alone as a signal for governmental responsiveness is that it does not account for the other side, or competing protest in the political arena. A greater number of activities conducted by movement behavior over countermovement protest can present an equally compelling case for why government should side with the more vociferous group. Lohmann (1995) and later King, Bentele, and Soule (2007) have analyzed governmental responsiveness by considering both sides of an issue space, but their measures omit consideration of the various social characteristics of protest.

These various measures have beneficial components that are derived from theoretical conceptions. As I argue in Chapter 1, including multiple factors in measuring protest events more closely mirrors the realities of non-electoral behavior. When information is available, politicians are likely to consider every aspect of minority protest.

Placing Minority Protest along a Continuum

Citizens' protest behavior is so multifaceted and complex that it would be impossible to create a perfect measure to capture it. It is possible, however, to build upon previous approaches to create a more encompassing measure. Accordingly, this work introduces a new measure of minority protest that considers the context of citizens' actions as well as competing concerns on minority issues.

First, I define "minority political protest" as collective behavior conducted by members of society who express a grievance that primarily relates to racial and ethnic minorities. These grievances address issues related to affirmative action, desegregation, voting rights, racial and ethnic discrimination in housing or employment, police brutality, and bicultural/bilingual education, among others. A complete list of grievances is provided in the appendix.

As for protest activities, I assess a wide range of citizen behavior, including demonstrations, rallies, marches, vigils, pickets, civil disobedience, information distribution, riots, strikes, and boycotts. I use a subset of events reported in the *New York Times* from 1960 through 1995 that are contained in the Dynamics of Collective Action (DCA) database, arguably the most comprehensive source on national protests events. Newspaper articles have become a "methodological staple" for studies of political protest (McAdam and Su 2002, 74). With the help of the DCP database, the *Times* has emerged as the most widely used newspaper source for analyzing the link between protest behavior and governmental action in quantitative studies (see, e.g., McAdam and Su 2002; Earl et al. 2003; King et al. 2007; Soule and Davenport 2009; Olzak and Soule 2009). Nevertheless, there are legitimate reasons to be concerned about limiting this analysis of protest activities to those mentioned in the *Times*. Christian Davenport

(2010), for example, analyzed various media stories on the Black Panther Party in the Bay Area and concluded that relying on only one media source presents a biased depiction of protest events. [1] I agree with the spirit of this critique but question whether the use of multiple news sources trades one potential problem for another.

The dilemma is that many papers did not cover minority protest in the early 1960s. In the South, many whites who were opposed to segregation lashed out against the media and created a climate of fear for reporters who were interested in covering the civil rights movement (Nelson 2003). Other news sources left coverage of minority protest to the Associated Press and were slow to establish bureaus in major southern cities. The *Washington Post*, for example, did not set up a bureau in Atlanta until 1970. And even some of the newspapers that were present in the South, such as the *Atlanta Constitution* and the *Atlanta Journal*, did not staff notorious events like the ones that transpired in Selma (Nelson 2003).

The *New York Times* was more proactive then other newspaper outlets when it came to covering minority protest. Jack Nelson, a Pulitzer Prize winner who is best known for his coverage of the civil rights movement and is former chief Washington correspondent for the *Los Angeles Times*, wrote, "The *[New York] Times* was far out front in covering the story, not only focusing on it long before other news organizations, but also devoting more resources and top news space to it and thereby helping make it part of the government's agenda" (2003, 7).

Including measures from multiple news sources, on the other hand, threatens to introduce a great deal of temporal variation, where one time period provides significantly more information than others. Indeed, this is what Davenport found when he examined media coverage of the Black Panthers. Temporal variation produces one type of bias, while focusing solely on the *New York Times* produces another stemming

[1] This bias is referred to as the "Rashomon Effect" (Davenport 2010).

from selection bias – disproportionately reporting events in a specific region of the United States. Thus, deciding to use one media source or multiple media sources becomes a matter of selecting the lesser of two evils.

Making use of the consistent measure of minority political protest offered by *New York Times* reporting is a more appealing approach to analyzing national responses, as assessing multiple newspaper sources would necessarily involve the inclusion of local media outlets that only certain federal politicians are likely to have read and been informed by. The underlying question guiding this book is whether government responds to racial and ethnic minority protest. Implicit in this question is the notion that politicians are aware of citizens' actions. If federal officials in national political institutions are not made aware of citizen concerns, they cannot respond to them. Lipsky (1968, 1151) put this best when he wrote, "Like a tree falling unheard in the forest, there is no protest unless protest is perceived and projected." Thus, the approach of including multiple newspaper sources would lead to a substantial underestimation of the regression coefficients, because there would be many local-level reports of protests that would not have been recognized by federal officials. The *New York Times*, in contrast, has a national distribution, making it more likely that national government officials would have been aware of minority protest events reported therein. [2]

In analyzing accounts in the *New York Times*, I go beyond merely examining whether or not a protest event occurred to explore the content of political behavior. I conceptualize

[2] Scholars have also argued that the *New York Times* will be less likely than the black press to report on the contentious nature of minority protest events (Davenport 2010; Weiner 2009). The conservative reports in the *Times*, however, would again underestimate the true effect of informative protest. If the *Times* had reported every minority protest event, this would likely provide greater information to politicians and amplify the influence of minority protest. (See Davenport et al. [2011, 158] for a similar point made on the subject of state repression.) Moreover, the reports in the *Times* should be considered as a proxy or a representative sample of the complete population of minority protests that a politician observed.

information in political protest in terms of levels of salience. Salient political behavior, and thus political behavior that delivers information to government officials, is defined as including any of the following: (1) protest activity that involves more than one hundred individuals, (2) protest activity that lasts more than a day, (3) protest activity that is supported by a political organization, (4) protest activity that results in property damage, (5) protest activity that draws a police presence, (6) protest activity that leads to an arrest, (7) protest activity that involves individuals carrying weapons, (8) protest activity that leads to injury, or (9) protest activity that involves death. I have transformed the nine definitions given above into binary variables and then summed across the binary variables to calculate a saliency score for each instance of protest. Computed in this fashion, a given protest event can have a saliency score that ranges from 0 to 9. To create an annual saliency score, I take all of the protest events that occurred in a particular year and aggregate their level of salience.[3]

After creating a saliency score, I then account for competing forces. To do this, I subtract the saliency scores of an anti-minority rights protest from those of its related pro-minority rights protest. What we are left with is a continuum for protest events in which positive values indicate a pro-minority-rights signal and negative values an anti-minority-rights signal.

This measure of protest captures some of the complexity of minorities' political behavior. First, it considers the diverse social conditions within racial and ethnic minority protest activities. Viewed in this manner, racial and ethnic minority protest can be conceived as being on a continuum, where higher scores indicate more informative events and scores that approach zero indicate uninformative behavior. Second, this measure builds upon previous designs by encompassing additional components of protest that affect its success or failure in influencing politicians.

[3] The saliency score is calculated as follows: $\textit{yearly salience} = \sum_{t-1}^{N} \textit{level of Salience}$, where N represents the total number of protest events in a year.

Perhaps the most useful aspect of this new measure is that it captures the direction of the political signal being sent to government. When the measure is positive, pro-minority voices are dominating the political arena; when it is negative, anti-minority rights protest is the louder voice. The measure also serves as an indicator of issue ownership. While competing sides will vie for attention from government, we can discern which side has more effectively embraced an issue as its own. Taken collectively, the new measure considers the scope of minority protest, which historians often capture but empirical studies tend to ignore.

The Layout and Trends of Informative Minority Protest

Having established a measure of minority protest, I can assess how the continuum of information it provides fluctuates in terms of issue ownership, geography, and time. It is unlikely that minority protest has provided constant, consistent information over the forty-year period under study. It is equally unlikely that salient minority protest was present throughout the nation. But where and when has minority protest overpowered counterprotest? Where and when were racial and ethnic minority concerns most often voiced?

Figure 2.1 plots the aggregate level of salience in pro-minority protest against the level of salience in anti-minority protest over the period 1960–95. Because the level of salience is aggregated for the entire year, the numbers are quite high. The largest gap appears at the height of the civil rights movement. This chasm remained into the late 1960s, when the Chicano movement was getting underway. But by the 1970s, the divide had closed, and the "tango" between opposing views had begun to take shape.

To better understand the relationship between these two sides, we can subtract anti-minority protest saliency scores from those of pro-minority protest. Figure 2.2 does just this by combining both lines in Figure 2.1 to indicate a pure pro-minority signal when the numbers are positive and a pure

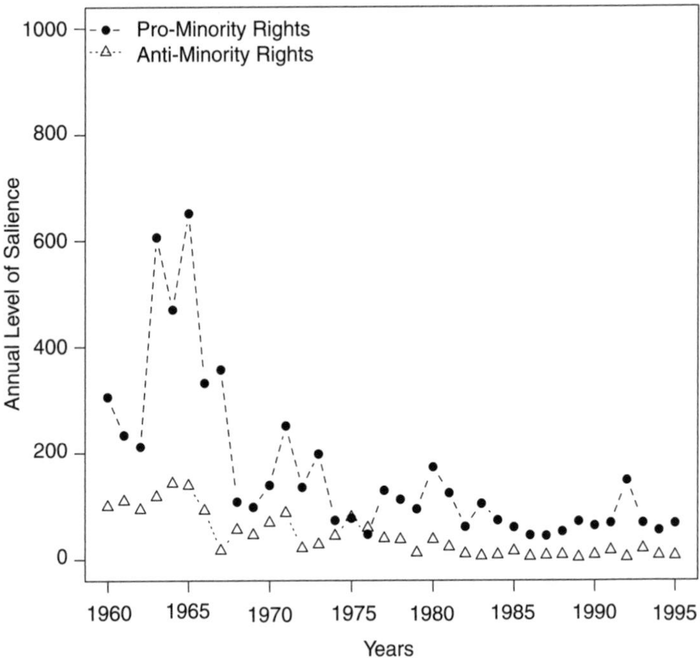

FIGURE 2.1. Competing voices, 1960–1995.

anti-minority signal when the numbers are negative. This figure offers a clearer historical picture of the signals that were being sent to government, as well as to citizens. Starting in 1963, the government was receiving a significantly strong signal in favor of minority concerns, and it is no coincidence that some of the most memorable moments of the civil rights movement occurred in this year. Protest events of 1963 included responses to the Sixteenth Street Baptist Church bombing, the integration of the University of Alabama, the events in Birmingham, and the March on Washington that included Martin Luther King's famous "I Have a Dream" address. These actions were followed by major legislative victories.

The passage of the Voting Rights Act in 1965 resulted in a decline in minority protest and an increase in white resentment that boosted anti-minority rights behavior. Hence, we see a considerable drop in the pro-minority signal strength

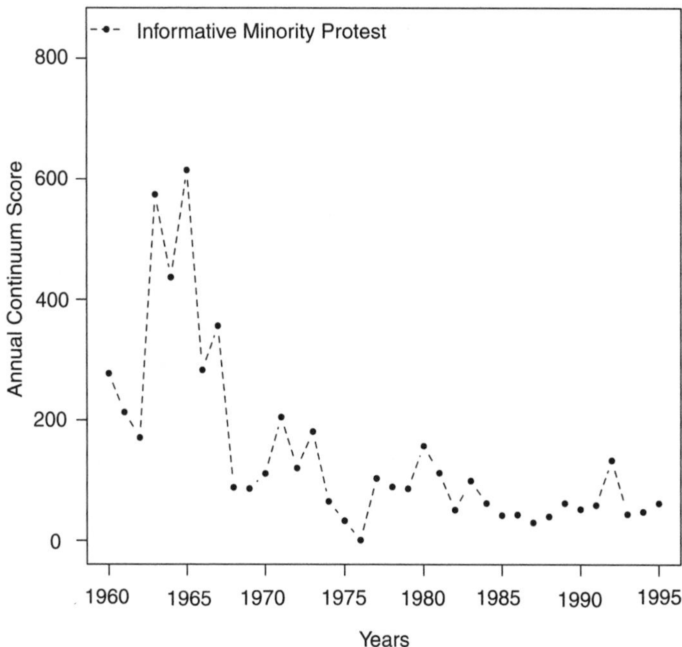

FIGURE 2.2. Information continuum of minority protest, 1960–1995.

in 1966. It rebounded slightly in 1967, when race riots in Newark, New Jersey, and Detroit, Michigan, combined with militant actions by the Black Panther Party to once again propel pro-minority concerns into the spotlight. The year 1968 marked the beginning of the lasting decline in pro-minority issue ownership on topics of race. The rhetoric associated with Richard Nixon's law-and-order presidential campaign helped to depress minority protest activities. By 1976, anti-minority-rights voices drowned out pro-minority appeals on race-related issues. Protest over affirmative action, quotas, and bussing captured the frustrations of many Americans who felt that progressive policies and rulings had gone too far. Ironically, these issues also stimulated engagement in protest activities by those who felt the policies did not go far enough. After 1980, pro-minority protest struggled to dominate the issue space. There was a slight increase in signal strength in 1988, when Jesse Jackson made his second bid for the presidency,

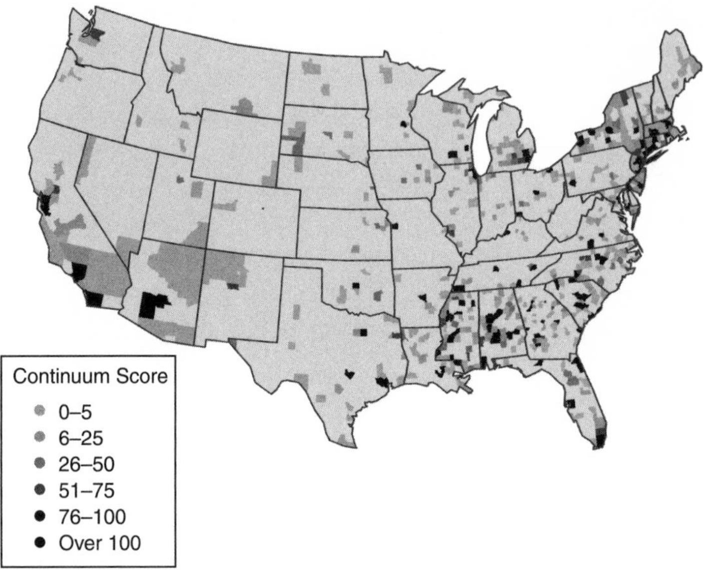

FIGURE 2.3. Informative minority protest across the United States, 1960–1995.

and a substantial increase in 1992 when the Rodney King riots rocked Los Angeles, but the overall trend has been downward since the mid-1960s, despite occasional spikes.

The information in minority protest fluctuated not only over time but also by location. To explore the geographical distribution, Figure 2.3 shows the average level of pro-minority protest across U.S. counties from 1960 through 1995. The darker-shaded areas indicate high levels of informative minority protest, while the lighter areas indicate less protest. One noticeable advantage to laying out the different geographical locations of informative protest is that it becomes easy to discern not only the origins of minority activity but also the intensity of minority political behavior. Figure 2.3 illustrates that minorities have made appeals throughout the nation. Unlikely locations, such as Hardin, Montana, and Rapid City, South Dakota, have experienced significant minority protest. Yet minority appeals are not equally voiced throughout the nation and vary drastically between counties.

There is a noticeable overlap between historical accounts of significant political protest and reporting of political protest in the *New York Times*. This is most evident in the South, where the concentration of minority protest in such places as Mobile, Alabama; Tupelo, Mississippi; and Columbia, South Carolina, reflects many of the tensions that existed South of the Mason-Dixie Line. On the West Coast and in the Northeast, protest events likely expressed multiracial concerns. The issues voiced in the Chicano and Asian American movements found a home in these geographical areas. The location of minority protest also captures much of the social unrest that took place in Newark, New Jersey; Rochester, New York; and later in Los Angeles, California.

While some areas clearly saw more political protest than others, the location of informative political behavior is well matched to our common expectations of where minority protest might arise. In particular, the geographical concentration of minority protest mirrors census identification of highly populated minority communities. While some level of spatial bias is expected, Figure 2.3 reveals that the *New York Times* coverage of minority protest events was not by any means limited to the Northeast, East Coast, or major metropolitan areas. In practice, we may never know the true spatial bias produced by using the *New York Times,* but the layout of protest from this source provides a good proxy of the signals being sent to government. It also indicates that federal officials from some areas were more informed about issues of race than other politicians.

The distribution of information provided by protest actions also varied over time. In Figure 2.4, informative signals are broken down by decade. In the 1960s, minority political protest was concentrated in major metropolitan cities and in the South. With the exception of California, the vast majority of signals of racial injustice converged on the East Coast. In the next decade, there were fewer signals stemming from minority protest activity, and the information was more dispersed. In the 1970s and 1980s, some neighborhoods in the West

Informative Minority Protests 1960s

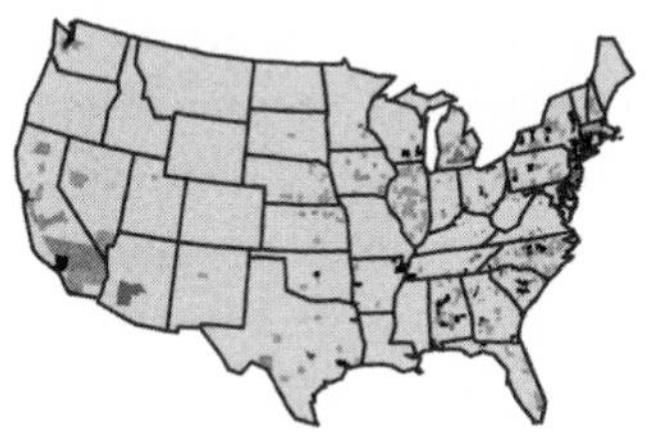

Informative Minority Protests 1970s

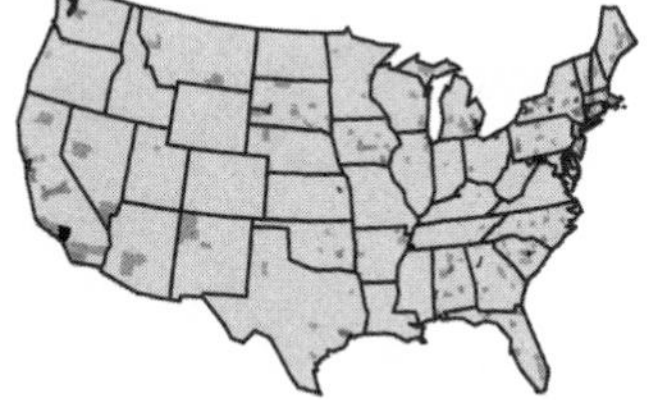

Informative Minority Protests 1980s

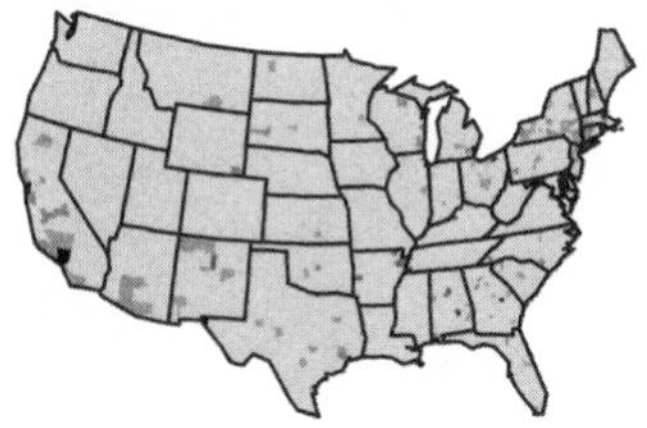

Informative Minority Protests 1990s

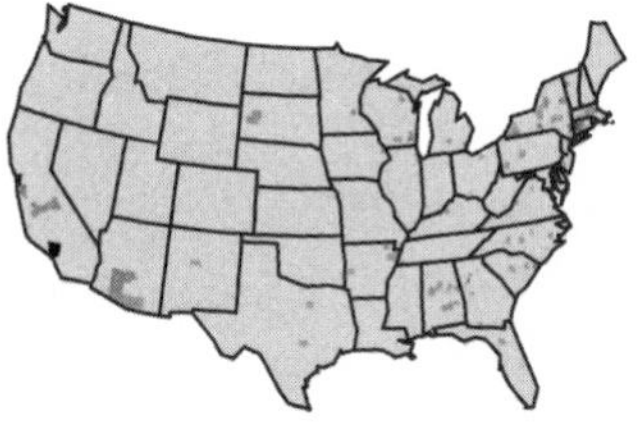

FIGURE 2.4. Location of minority protests (1960s, 1970s, 1980s, and 1990s).

Coast and Midwest witnessed minority appeals directly for the first time. As protest expanded and moved to other parts of the nation, bystanders were able to see the social context of political actions firsthand, becoming personally familiar with the issues being voiced through minority activity.[4]

Minority Protest and the Public's Changing Attitudes on Racial Issues

This observation about the geographical layout of informative protests points to a socialization component of political activism. Just as minority political behavior may affect

[4] Though protest became less informative over the period studied, the issues gradually reached more individuals. The important point here is that if protest had decreased and remained concentrated in one place, it would have less influence than protest that decreased and spread out.

governmental officials, average Americans could also take note of the information protest provides and allow it to influence their decisions. Onlookers can use the information in minority protest to make voting decisions (Lohmann 1995). Similar to strategic voting, in which citizens punish or reward politicians with their vote on the basis of economic indicators, the scope of political protest may influence how citizens cast their ballots. It may also change the way the public views political issues. If minority protest activities are salient enough, they may rise in importance on the public agenda.

This brings us back to the question of what role, if any, public opinion plays in the relationship between minority political protest and government action. It could potentially mediate the attention government pays to racial issues. But public opinion is created, formed, and, in some rare cases, sustained over time. Thus, while the information in political protest may directly shape the decisions of federal officials, the cues in political behavior may also produce a favorable environment of public opinion to facilitate governmental response.

The claim that minority protest actions can influence citizens' perceptions of racial and ethnic minority concerns is at odds with arguments that public opinion is formed from the top down. The top-down theory of public opinion argues that political elites shape and drive public perceptions (Converse 1964; Sniderman 2000; Zaller 1992). According to this argument, the complexity of issues forces citizens to rely on political specialists for information. John Zaller cements this top-down process as a fixture in understanding public opinion formation. He states that when elites divide on an issue, citizens will tend to follow the views of those elites "sharing their general ideological or partisan predisposition" (1992, 9).

But it is difficult to conceive a top-down process at work in the government's response to twentieth-century racial and ethnic minority concerns. It was citizens, not political elites, who brought minority issues to the forefront through the civil rights, Chicano, and Asian American movements. Many political leaders minimized their discussions of race or avoided race all together. Presidents Eisenhower and Kennedy, for example, were forced to address race only after citizens' contentious political actions became impossible to ignore (Riley 1999). Consequently, it is not surprising to find that Lee's work (2002) questions the operation of the top-down process in race relations. Lee contends that the influence that stems from the connection between citizens' political behavior and their policy preferences is stronger than the one between elites and citizens' preferences (69). If Lee's argument is correct, then information originating from minority protest should be strongly associated with fluctuations in public opinion views on race-related issues.

Public opinion, at least theoretically, is the collective belief of the public regarding the major issues to be resolved in society. In order to examine whether issues of race are increasing in importance in the eye of the public at the same time that minority protest is becoming more informative, I turn to the Gallup Poll's Most Important Problem (MIP) series. The Gallup Poll's MIP Series is one of the longest-standing measures of the public agenda. The question "What do you consider to be the most important problem facing America today?" has been used to address the relevance of particular issues over time (McCombs and Zhu 1995). When the percentage of individuals who feel race or race relations is the most important problem facing the country today increases, I consider this an indication that racial issues have become more important on the public agenda. I take the average of all the surveys conducted in a given year to offer an annual percentage. In Figure 2.5, I again plot the annual continuum of minority protest scores, this time overlapping this trend with the percentage of individuals who felt that race relations were the most important problems facing the nation at the time they were polled. The fluctuation in national attitudes on race frequently mimics the trend of minority protest. The similarities are undeniable for 1963, 1967, 1975, and 1992, years where drastic increases or decreases took place.

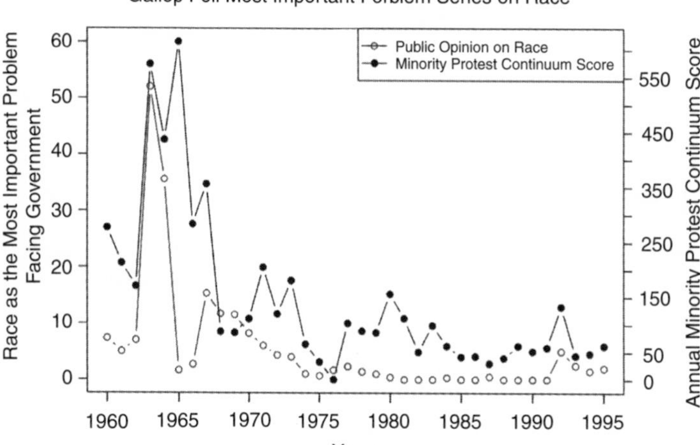

FIGURE 2.5. Public perceptions of race as an important problem facing the nation alongside informative minority protest.

To more rigorously test this association, I assess the impact of salient minority protest against other competing factors that may have influenced public perceptions on race. The results, compiled in Table 2.1, confirm that minorities' political protest actions have a significant impact on public opinion that views race as an important issue. When a higher level of minority protest action occurs, it is associated with a larger percentage of the nation feeling that racial or ethnic concerns are the nation's most important problem.[5]

Table 2.1 considers three alternate explanations for the nation's attention to racial issues: the nation's involvement in war, the level of unemployment, and the number of minority members of Congress. War influences attitudes about race in a negative direction. Citizens become less alarmed about minority grievances during periods of war, most likely because

[5] For example, in a year where there is an average continuum protest score, 263, this results in at least 7.9 percent of the nation feeling that racial or ethnic concerns are the most important problems facing America today. This is a substantial increase, given that any one issue rarely makes it beyond 2–3 percent of the nation feeling that it is the most important problem facing the nation.

TABLE 2.1. *Factors that influence the emergence of racial issues as an important problem facing the nation*

Public Opinion on Race		Pr(>|t|)
Lagged Dependent	0.2740 (0.1678)	0.1137
Minority Protest$_t$	0.0360*** (0.0076)	0.0001
Minority Protest$_{t-1}$	−0.0113 (0.0093)	0.2337
Periods of War	−5.8055† (3.1430)	0.0753
Minorities in Congress	−0.0563 (0.1827)	0.7601
Unemployment Rate	−1.3460 (0.8887)	0.1411
N	34	
R^2	.6459	
adj. R^2	.570	
F-statistic	8.511	
p-value	.00002	

Notes: The dependent variable indicates the percentage of individuals in the nation who feel that racial and ethnic minority concerns are the most important problems that government should address. Statistical Significance is denoted as follows: significant at $^{\dagger}p < .10$; $^{*}p < .05$; $^{**}p < .01$; $^{***}p < .001$.

Source: Public perceptions of race are drawn from Gallup Poll Most Important Problem (MIP) series (1960–1995).

international concerns deter the American public from thinking about domestic issues. Other national trends, such as low unemployment, do not distract the public's attention from minority concerns. Finally, one might expect that the number of minorities in Congress would influence racial attitudes by pushing them higher on the public's agenda. This form of elite influence has little sway over public opinion, however.

This examination reveals that the American public recognizes the informative cues that stem from minority protest actions, perhaps even before national governmental institutions have an opportunity to respond. The implications of this conclusion are significant. The link between public opinion and governmental action is already well documented.[6] But what this examination shows is that national perceptions, much of which government follows, are in part driven by political behavior. This suggests that minority political behavior may produce the environment it needs to be successful *and* later work within this environment to influence political actors.

Plan of Analysis

In order to incorporate the conclusion that political protest influences public opinion on race into the research design, I use the results in Table 2.1 as the first stage in a two-stage process, taking the predicted values of public opinion estimated by the results in Table 2.1 as a new variable of public perceptions in the remaining chapters. The inclusion of this variable allows for an examination of how national attitudes on race that have been influenced by the information in political protest are subsequently able to impact government. By considering the predicted values of public opinion alongside minority political activism, I am able to discern both the direct and the indirect impact of an information continuum of protest.

In the chapters that follow, I have chosen not to specify the exact timing between when the inception of a protest event began and the moment at which a governmental response occurred. Rather than restrict the model so that protest will have a constrained effect at a particular lag, I distribute the

[6] Public opinion is described as having much sway on political institutions (Wlezien 2004). The will of the people permeates each branch of government. Congressional leaders stay attuned to public opinion and are beholden to their districts (Miller and Stokes 1963, Page and Shapiro 1983; Stimson et al. 1995; Erikson et al. 1993; Monroe 1998; Hartley and Russett 1992, Achen 1975, Bartels 1991, among others). Presidents, likewise, respond to overall public opinion (Geer 1996; Canes-Wrone and Shotts 2004; Canes-Wrone et al. 2001). And Supreme Court justices have been shown to follow a general public mood (Mishler and Sheehan 1993), though the impact of public opinion varies by issue (Flemming and Wood 1997).

lags to analyze the lasting impact of minority protest. In doing so, I argue that political protest that occurs in the present will continue to have an effect on future governmental action, though the impact will decrease geometrically. To capture this concept, I use an autoregressive distributed lagged (ADL) model to analyze each federal institution in Chapters 3, 4, and 5.

Conclusion

The new measure of minority protest presented in this chapter indicates the varying level of information that citizens' actions provide and also captures competing protest events that attempt to garner the attention of government. This directional measure of pro-minority protest is key to understanding the governmental responses featured in the three chapters that follow. Government officials are not only able to see the content of specific events, but they are also likely to link these political events to other protest behavior that has occurred around the given issue. My measure of political protest encompasses these considerations.

This chapter has also explored the trends and geographical location of the salient information in minority protest events. We find that pro-minority protest concerns were more likely to be expressed during periods identified as movements, and their frequency has declined over time. Likewise, public perceptions of the importance of racial issues have become less salient. These two trends parallel one another, with minority protest helping to change racial attitudes.

In the three chapters that follow, I assess the influence that the minority protest information continuum has on each branch of the federal government. I also explore whether minority protest actions have been heightened by a salient atmosphere of public opinion.

3

Viewing Minority Protest from the Hill

The Individual and Collective Response from Congress

> *The anger that you see expressed out there in Los Angeles, in my district this evening, is a righteous anger, and it's difficult for me to say to the people, "Don't be angry."*
>
> – *Representative Maxine Waters (D-CA)*

The signals from minority protest have become weaker and more dispersed throughout the nation. As the context of minority protest has changed over time, so too have national political institutions transformed since the 1960s. Congress in particular has experienced a significant change in the demographic makeup of elected representatives. The early 1970s ushered in a wave of black and Latino legislators, many of whom emerged from the protest activities of the 1960s. The two major political parties also grew in importance and began exercising more influence over their representatives in Congress, pushing members to make stronger appeals to racial and ethnic minority voters. These changes created an environment in which minority protest appeals, though declining in salience, nonetheless retained strong potential to resonate.

As the "people's institution" of government, Congress is the branch perhaps most apt to be responsive to the political actions of engaged citizens. However, it can be difficult to assess congressional responsiveness. The LA riots of 1992 and the subsequent governmental response by Representative Maxine Waters demonstrate that protest conveys information to representatives at both district and national levels. As this case study will suggest, it is the protests that originate within a given representative's district that are the true catalysts for changing the behavior of congressional leaders, as opposed to those occurring elsewhere.

But not all districts are the same. Some districts have large populations of racial and ethnic minorities, and scholars have shown that these demographic anomalies engender the representatives that reside in them to support minority policies. Yet we should be careful not to overlook an important distinction: the difference between an active minority population and inactive minority population. Large populations of African Americans, Latinos, and Asian Americans residing in a district does not always equate to the elected representative of that district championing policies that benefit racial and ethnic minorities. Even congressional districts with populations that are predominantly minority must alert their representatives of the unique concerns affecting their community for those issues to be addressed. While the racial background of representatives and their political party affiliation mediate whether these concerns are consistent with national party platforms and personal beliefs, the scope of minority protest behavior also directs their individual actions.

Considering the Collective and the Individual

Congress is the only national branch of government that consists of individuals whose task it is to address the unique goals of a specific geographic location. This orientation benefits citizens who seek to make appeals for the redress of racial injustices. Congressional leaders can focus on the information communicated by protest events from their own districts or states rather than consider the national landscape of political behavior. Thus, it would seem natural to assume that members of Congress draw on political protest for information about critical issues and that their voting records are shaped by the social context of protest in their districts.

Scholarly research has struggled, however, to establish a direct link between minority protest and congressional voting behavior. For example, Burstein (1998) shows that minority demonstrations were ineffective in influencing the passage of equal employment opportunity legislation. The lack of evidence for the influence of protest on the behavior of individual congressional representatives even goes beyond studies of race. Scholarship has shown that the political protests of the women's suffrage movement were unsuccessful in influencing congressional voting (King et al. 2005), and women's overall collective behavior did not win congressional votes on gender issues (Soule et al. 1999). With the exception of a few (McAdam and Su 2002; Santoro 2002), scholars have generally concluded that citizens' political protest activities have little effect on congressional actions (Soule et al. 1999).

Given the mission of members of Congress to represent the American people, one might wonder why studies have failed to demonstrate a direct link between political protest and congressional policies. The type of attention Congress can offer likely explains this enigma. Members of Congress may express their attention to protest signals individually, or the aggregate body may react. When it comes to political issues troubling minority communities, these two forms of response will not always be in sync with one another. Some individual members of Congress will be attentive to strong information signals coming from minority protest but later have their individual votes overshadowed by the collective voice of an unaffected House of Representatives. The unrelenting will of certain members of Congress to ignore the information stemming from minority protest, on the other hand, may be overcome by the collective's desire to address racial inequality. Both forms of responsiveness can indicate how receptive Congress is to the signaling strength of minority protest.

Most examinations of Congress focus on the aggregate level of response. In doing so, they establish a fragile connection between nationwide protest activity and collective congressional responses. This might seem rational at face value, but why should a representative from Wichita, Kansas, be concerned about minority protest occurring in Philadelphia, Pennsylvania? The optimistic response might be that representatives are concerned about every form of injustice, holding true to the words of Martin Luther King that an "injustice anywhere is a threat to justice everywhere." While King's words may be true, the actions of representatives are not purely motivated by this sanguine notion. Preponderant evidence indicates congressional leaders are most concerned about their own constituents and the social conditions in their districts.

In some cases, representatives vote on policies desired by their constituents because they share the interests of these constituents, in a situation Harold Gosnell (1948) refers to as "unconscious representation." Even when politicians do not share the interests of their constituents, however, the goal of reelection constrains their voting patterns to follow the preferences of their districts (Mayhew 1974). Richard Fenno's work illustrates that "[i]f you get too far away from your district, you'll lose it" (1978, 148). Legislators look within their districts and become attuned to their constituents to understand the relevance of all issues, including minority concerns. This behavior is best exemplified by the aftermath of the 1965 Voting Rights Act, which eliminated many of the barriers that prevented minorities from participating in elections and increased their political participation. As the number of minority voters increased in many southern districts, several southern Democrats in Congress shifted their support in favor of civil rights issues (Black 1978, 448–49; Stern 1985, 114).[1]

[1] The majority of white congressional members from the South supported the final passage of 1975 amendments to several civil rights bills – the first time since Reconstruction that this occurred (McDonald 1992). This speaks to a

Congressional leaders could be attuned to political protest expressing minority concerns that occurs within their respective districts much as they are attuned to shifts in the minority makeup of the district or the demographics of their electorate. The social characteristics of minority protest are likely to alert politicians of a critical issue in their district that is rising in importance. When these protest actions largely stem from one side of the issue space, they can also offer a coherent understanding of protesters' specific grievances and inform politicians of the right course of action. Indeed, this was the case for protest events that occurred in Los Angeles, California, in 1992.

The LA Riots and District-Level Information

On March 3, 1991, Rodney King led police officers on a high-speed car chase. When he finally brought his vehicle to a stop, the officers at the scene requested that he get out of the car and lay on the ground. King refused to obey the officers' commands, and he was consequently tasered, beaten fifty-six times with "forceful blows," and arrested. The episode left King with twenty stitches, a broken cheekbone, a broken right ankle, and eleven skull fractures.[2] In a fortuitous turn of events, and unbeknownst to the officers who made the arrest, the incident was recorded on videotape by George Holliday, a civilian who taped the footage from his apartment across the street. The next day, the video aired on the local television station, KTLA. The shocking footage showed four Los Angeles police officers, all white, beating and kicking King, an African American.

Within a week, the four officers involved in the incident had been indicted by a grand jury on charges of using excess force and committing assault with a deadly weapon.

larger point: as minorities have played a greater part in the political system, they have received greater representation and more favorable policy (Whitby and Gilliam 1991).

[2] King also alleged that he had suffered permanent kidney and brain damage.

However, a jury of ten white citizens, one Hispanic, and one Asian American acquitted three of the officers and partially acquitted the fourth. Within hours of the decision, roughly three hundred protesters had gathered outside the Simi Valley Courthouse. The protest soon turned violent, sparking a two-day period in which buildings burned to the ground, property was damaged, citizens clashed with local and federal officials, and numerous arrests took place.

Many in the media described these protest events as looting and rioting running rampant in the streets. Though the protest events affected various locations in Los Angeles, the majority were located in the Twenty-Ninth Congressional District of California, which encompasses South Central Los Angeles. The congressional representative from that district, Maxine Waters (D-CA), did not perceive the protest actions as rioting: "If you call it a riot it sounds like it was just a bunch of crazy people who went out and did bad things for no reason. I maintain it was somewhat understandable, if not acceptable. So I call it a rebellion."

Political protest actions occurred specifically in Representative Waters' district, and she was urged to respond. She did so not because she felt troubled that an escalation of protest activity would lead to chaos, though she acknowledged the contentious environment, or because she felt that public opinion might be sympathetic to the rioters. It was not.[3] Rather, her response was an acknowledgement of the information being voiced through the protest actions. The extremism of these actions only illuminated how dire was the need to address minority concerns in South Central. In an interview with *Ebony* magazine immediately following the Rodney King protests, Waters stated her view that the protesters' actions were rooted in "years of neglect of America's inner cities." She went on to draw links to employment. More importantly,

[3] While Representative Waters did not condone the violence seen the in riots, she was not ready to denounce the events, as her colleagues in Congress had already done. She stated afterward that she was not "going to be a caricature of some 1960s Black leader, saying, 'Cool it, baby, cool it'" (Collier 1992, 36).

she stated that these political actions served the purpose of informing a less knowledgeable Congress: "It's about neglect. I have known for quite some time that the growing numbers of young Black and Latino males who are unemployed were going to be a structural problem for America. We are working with a Congress that has no understanding of what's wrong with America.... It takes things like this rebellion to wake people up" (40).

In the months following the riots in LA, Waters's behavior on Capitol Hill changed. Waters had just recently arrived to Washington and thus had an abbreviated voting record, but her previous roll-call votes demonstrated a strong pro-minority stance. After the protests in LA, she took an even stronger position on race by voting in the liberal direction on every minority bill for the remainder of the 103rd congressional session. She also began to set the agenda in Congress by bringing new issues to the House floor. In the session prior to the riots, Waters introduced bills that focused on Veteran benefits, debt-collection practices, the empowerment of women in foreign countries, and grants to help at-risk youth.[4] Waters considered these issues important topics that she should address. After the riots, the bills she introduced focused more on minority employment. She introduced H.R. 4159, which "encouraged gainful employment among the residents of public housing." In the session following the riots, Waters continued to introduce legislation targeted to minority employment with the following bills: H.R. 1021, the Neighborhood Infrastructure Improvement and Inner City Job Creation Act, and H.R. 1020, Jobs and Life Skills Improvement. These bills were novel, and they attempted to remedy the problems Waters believed were at the root of the protest events.

The response of Representative Waters went beyond the floor of the House. Waters was also determined to be involved

[4] See H.R. 4967 (veteran benefits), H.R. 6207 (debt-collection practices), H.R. 6208 (women empowerment), and H.R. 6210 (grants to help at-risk youth).

in closed-door discussions about the events in her district. George H. W. Bush assembled various congressional leaders and Cabinet members to discuss the aftermath of the Rodney King events. His decision to do so illustrates the ability of the executive office to receive signals from protest actions and respond to these events in both public and private settings – a point I will leave to the next chapter. Waters was not invited to attend this discussion session with the president. This did not prevent her from appearing at the White House door and demanding to be involved in the discussion, however. As Waters expected, she was allowed to attend. At the meeting, she expressed her constituents' grievances and suggested new policies to address them.[5]

In the wake of the LA riots, then, the governmental response from Maxine Waters was direct, immediate, and forceful. The impetus for this response was derived from the social context of minority protest actions. Political protest informed Waters of the urgency of a number of important problems dealing with inner-city problems and unemployment, and it opened up a space for policy innovation to address them. The intense saliency, driven by the contentious nature of events, sent cues that Waters ought to give these issues higher priority than other problems affecting the South Central area. And finally, the overwhelming number of protests stemming from one side of the issue space informed Waters that she should take a position supportive of minority concerns. Waters acquired the information she needed to address the concerns of her constituents in ways she and they believed would improve governance.

In comparison to Waters, the actions of other members in the House of Representatives in response to the LA protest events were negligible. To be fair, some of these issues, such as unemployment, were region-specific and applied only to a

[5] Maria Newman, "After the Riots: Washington at Work; Lawmaker From Riot Zone Insists on a New Role for Black Politicians," *New York Times*, May 19, 1992.

limited number of congressional districts. But the difference between Waters's response and those of her congressional colleagues also speaks to the unique nature of the legislative branch to mediate the information in political protest. Though congressional leaders are national politicians, they are most beholden to those whom they represent. The protest events surrounding Rodney King were no different. Thus, the information in district-level protest actions sent signals focused on district-level problems.

There appear, then, to be two congressional spheres of potential influence: political actions that occur within a representative's district and those that exist in the national political arena. If this is the case, then we should expect to observe a difference in how Congress as a collective responds to minority protest versus how the same protest affects individual legislators' voting records.

A Collective Response from the House of Representatives

The insights offered by the LA riots strengthen the expectation that as a collective body, Congress is unlikely to respond to national protest events. But perhaps there are responses from the legislative body that can be observed at different stages of the policy-making process. Thus, to gauge the collective response of Congress to minority protest, I consider both hearings and legislation. This approach allows us to examine legislative behavior from the beginning of the policy-making process, when congressional hearings are held, to the end: the passage of laws.

The congressional hearing is an important tool for analyzing symbolic responsiveness in Congress. Hearings have offered scholars valuable insight into the jurisdiction of congressional committees (Baumgartner et al. 2000). Bills that are of sufficient importance are able to obtain public hearings, which serve as a measure to determine which issues Congress deems critical. Even nonlegislative hearings are important to consider, because these activities lead to the renaming of issues, which changes the committee that can claim jurisdiction over them (Talbert et al. 1995, 5).

Minority organizations have long used congressional hearings as a platform to voice their political preferences. Not surprisingly, congressional hearings on racial and ethnic minority concerns increased in the early 1960s, and this increase closely paralleled an influx in interest-group campaigning around discrimination and civil-rights issues (Meyer et al. 2005, 70). Given that the committees that introduce and oversee these public forums can be influenced by outside pressure (Polsby 1968; Ragsdale and Theis 1997), hearings should serve as a good measure of congressional responsiveness. This may be understood as "symbolic responsiveness," however, because hearings activity does not directly change policy.

Analysis of congressional behavior reveals that symbolic responsiveness is plentiful. Hearings are held often, and they cover a large range of issues. But hearings rarely lead to the passage of laws, and they therefore produce little or no change in the lives of the individuals who initially voiced the concerns. Thus, symbolic responsiveness provides a wealth of information on congressional actions, but it is not equivalent to direct policy responsiveness.

Congress acts most directly through the passage of new laws, the purest form of public policy. In spite of this, or perhaps because of it, the probability of any bill becoming law is minute. The number of laws enacted in any given year is small, and the number of laws enacted around minority concerns even smaller. The minority legislation that has passed, however, such as the civil rights legislation of 1965 and 1968, exercises a significant and sustained impact on social conditions in America, and in some cases has set the foundation for future legislation. I refer to the passage of legislation as "substantive responsiveness." I define "minority responsiveness" as congressional response to discrimination, immigration, and the education of underprivileged students, as well as congressional provision for welfare programs and assistance to low-income families, by means of any of the symbolic or

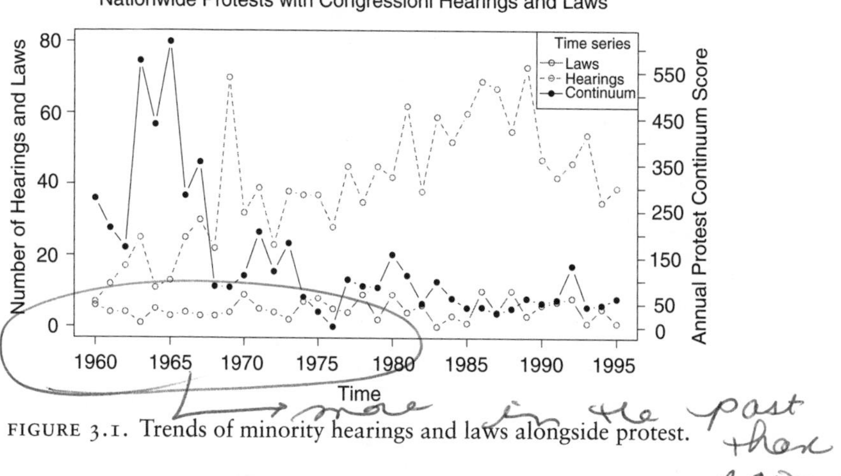

FIGURE 3.1. Trends of minority hearings and laws alongside protest.

substantive approaches highlighted previously. I draw data on both symbolic and substantive responses from the Policy Agendas Project.

When we examine annual trends in Figure 3.1, we find that neither symbolic hearings nor substantive laws tracked informative minority behavior, which is captured by an annual protest continuum score.[6] Each trend took a divergent path. Congressional hearings on racial and ethnic minority concerns have become more frequent over time, reflecting a tendency in Congress to more readily address minority issues through hearings. The peak year for hearings was 1969, when Congress held seventy-nine hearings on minority issues. As expected, the number of laws passed affecting racial and ethnic minority concerns was consistently lower than the number of hearings held, dropping to zero in 1983 and never rising above ten (in 1986 and 1988) in any given year. Moreover, the number of minority laws produced over time does not reveal

[6] Recall that the minority protest continuum score is created by first adding the various social characteristics of protest to reach a salience score for each event. I then subtract the annual level of salience of anti-minority rights protests from pro-minority rights protests to obtain a minority protest continuum score for each year.

any sort of trend. While there were significant increases in the late 1970s and 1980s, the pattern appears stagnant.

The overall trend of the relationship between congressional hearings and informative political protest does not converge or overlap. As hearings increased over time, political protest decreased. This negative relationship is most prevalent for 1968, a year many would consider to be the endpoint of the civil rights movement. During the civil rights period, the relationship was slightly positive. On several occasions, the number of minority hearings mimics the ebbs and flows seen in the social content of political protest.

The relationship between protest behavior and the passage of legislation has also changed over time. Before 1970, the passage of laws affecting minorities did not respond to changes in protest activity. Ironically, as the number of salient political actions dropped significantly after 1970, fluctuations in the passage of minority laws started to mimic changes in political protest: even slight increases in political protest were followed by increases in congressional legislation. But these relationships – between political behavior and minority hearings, as well as between behavior and minority laws – are convoluted. Figure 3.1 does not reveal a distinguishable pattern of influence.

To offer more clarity on whether these previous patterns are systematically related, I employ an autoregressive distributed lagged (ADL) model, a statistical technique to understand the association of historical trends. This statistical model also allows us to consider alternative explanations for shifts in the number of minority hearings held in Congress and the passage of minority-related laws. For example, Congress may be less productive on all issues when there is divided government, that is, when a political party other than the president's controls either or both chambers of Congress. On the other hand, the presence of a greater number of congressional members in the House of Representatives who identify as a racial or ethnic minority could increase the number of minority-friendly hearings held and laws passed, given that minority representatives

TABLE 3.1. *Factors that influence minority hearings and laws*

	Hearings	Laws
Lagged Dependent Variable	0.171	−0.323*
	(0.187)	(0.190)
Minority Protest$_t$	0.030	−0.004
	(0.047)	(0.010)
Minority Protest$_{t-1}$	−0.050*	−0.002
	(0.028)	(0.006)
Public Opinion$_t$	−0.485	−0.004
	(0.422)	(0.090)
Public Opinion$_{t-1}$	−0.867	0.005
	(0.752)	(0.162)
Divided Government$_t$	−4.741	0.922
	(6.453)	(1.375)
Minorities in Congress$_t$	−0.187	−0.063
	(0.365)	(0.077)
Civil Rights Movement$_t$	−1.536	−0.728
	(12.904)	(2.759)
N	35	35
R^2	0.549	0.202

Notes: Statistical Significance is denoted as follows: significant at *p < .05; **p < .01; ***p < .001. Data on minority laws was compiled from the *Policy Agendas Project.*

have been shown to advocate for minority issues. Finally, we can also examine whether Congress was more active during the post–civil rights era, as the previous figures indicate. In Table 3.1, I consider the impact that minority political protest has had on congressional behavior in relation to competing explanations.

The results show that few variables serve to explain rises in the frequency of minority hearings and the passage of minority laws by Congress. It would seem that increases in the national level of minority protest did not inform the legislature as a collective body. Ironically, salient protest levels, which are lagged by one year, *decreased* the number of minority hearings. The results are quite sobering, but they do echo the conclusions reached by previous works: collective minority protest actions are not influencing a unified response from Congress.

Although these results are somewhat disconcerting, there is a silver lining. The research design that examines Congress as a unified body does not correspond with real world events seen by congressional members' reaction to the Los Angeles riots. Maxine Waters's response to the events in Los Angeles suggests that legislators might be more attentive to the social environment of minority protests that occur in their own districts. The section that follows tests this proposition.

Individual Representatives' Responses

A representative's voting record is an appropriate means to understand whether congressional leaders are responsive to the social content of political protest that occurs within their districts. Examining congressional roll-call votes on racial and ethnic minority concerns is not an easy task, however. Consider, for example, a vote to continue debate on funding a welfare program. A "nay" vote may indicate that a representative believes there is still relevant material to discuss before the bill can succeed at the next stage in the policy-making process, or it may be a stall tactic imposed by representatives who wish to block the legislation. In this case, a "nay" vote could be interpreted as favorable or unfavorable for racial and ethnic minorities. As more complicated topics are introduced, it becomes difficult for researchers to differentiate supporters from opponents of minority legislation on the basis of roll-call voting. Thus, conclusions drawn from this subjective approach are likely to vary, and results are susceptible to bias. To overcome this problem, I implement two well-known measures of congressional members' ideology on minority issues.

The first measure is Clinton, Jackman, and Rivers's widely used technique of creating ideal point estimates. Ideal point estimates are values that indicate how liberal or conservative politicians are on a specific issue. The process of creating ideal points derives from the basic space theory of ideology. The underlying idea of this method is that legislators' votes are likely grouped across issues. In essence, a representative who votes favorably for welfare programs will also cast favorable votes for affirmative action or increasing urban housing development. Thus, knowing a representative's vote on one or two issues indicates how a representative will vote on other issues (Converse 1964). This technique uses spatial models to geometrically place politicians within a Euclidean space, where each representative has a preferred policy. This preferred policy can be conceived as a representative's ideal point. This point is unknown before the representative casts a vote. Though when representatives vote "yea" or "nay" on roll-call votes, they reveal more information about the location of their preferred ideal point.

Using established classifications of minority roll-call votes by Rohde (2010) and Poole and Rosenthal (1997), I narrow the votes in the House of Representatives to only those dealing with racial and ethnic minority concerns and create an ideal point.[7] Interpreting standard ideal point estimates can be complex. To ease interpretation, I first invert the point estimates, so that higher values indicate a more liberal position and lower values a more conservative stance. This way, positive values mean congressional leaders are supporting a bill favored by racial and ethnic minorities, while negative values indicate they are unsupportive. Second, I use only the ordinal properties of the ideal point to rank-order the representatives and give each legislator a liberal position score. Since the ranks are determined by comparing one legislator's vote on a race-related roll-call vote against that of another, the ordering is based upon the specific Congress in which a representative served. While this method cannot tell us how liberal a politician is in absolute terms, it can inform us of a legislator's liberal voting record on minority policies in relation to other members in the House of Representatives. For example, if a representative receives a position score of 80, this means that she is more liberal on minority issues than 80 percent of other

[7] A complete list of the issue codes can be found in the appendix.

members in the House and less liberal on minority issues than 20 percent of her colleagues.

As a secondary measure, I use Leadership Conference on Civil Rights (LCCR) scores. This is also a measure that indicates how liberal or conservative politicians are on a specific issue. Biannually, the LCCR collects only a few key roll-call votes that it deems determinant of whether representatives are supportive of both liberal and civil rights issues. Scholars have widely used these scores to understand legislators' positions on race (see Swain 1993; Whitby 1987, 1997; Bullock 1981; and Lublin 1997). Unfortunately, LCCR did not begin to collect information on roll-call votes until 1972. Given that the analysis in this work examines political protest from 1960, a significant period of time cannot be reviewed using LCCR scores. Another difficulty in using LCCR scores is that the votes that the score encompasses include some bills that are unrelated to minority issues. Bills covering issues on gender rights, disability, and the elderly can also be included in the calculation of LCCR scores. Thus, while LCCR scores heavily focus on minority issues, the introduction of unrelated topics will dilute the accuracy of the scores as representations of a legislator's stance on race. Even given these potential drawbacks, the LCCR score provides a useful measure to assess a legislator's position on race alongside nominate scores.

Both measures – ideal point estimates and LCCR scores – are highly correlated with informative minority protest actions that are placed along an information continuum. Starting with legislators' ideal point positions in Figure 3.2, I match the level of minority protest that occurs in a district with a representative's voting record on minority bills. More specifically, I group the continuum scores of congressional districts into various ranges on the *y*-axis. On the *x*-axis, I indicate the corresponding ideal point position, which is the average score for all the legislators clustered in a specific range. The relationship between protest and liberal positions is startling. Minority protests exhibiting higher continuum scores are associated with more liberal ideal point estimates. This

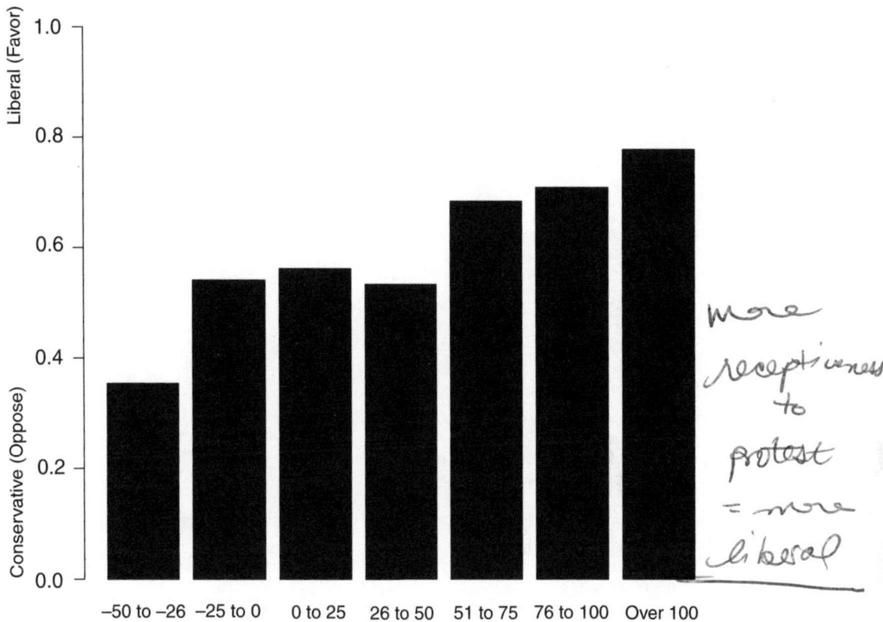

FIGURE 3.2. Individual congressional roll-call votes and ideal point scores on racial and ethnic minority concerns, 1960–1995.

indicates that congressional leaders were more likely to vote liberal on minority issues when moderate and contentious social characteristics of political protest informed politicians of the scope of minority activism and when pro-minority rights protests overshadowed appeals from anti-minority rights activism within a representative's district. The association between liberal votes and informative minority protest is even more astonishing once the continuum score for minority protest passes one hundred in any given district. When the scope of protest activity becomes this informative, legislators from these districts are likely to be more liberal on minority issues than 80 percent of their colleagues.

The relationship between minority protest and legislators' liberal LCCR scores is also strong. In Figure 3.3, the *x*-axis on the scatter plot is the average continuum score for minority

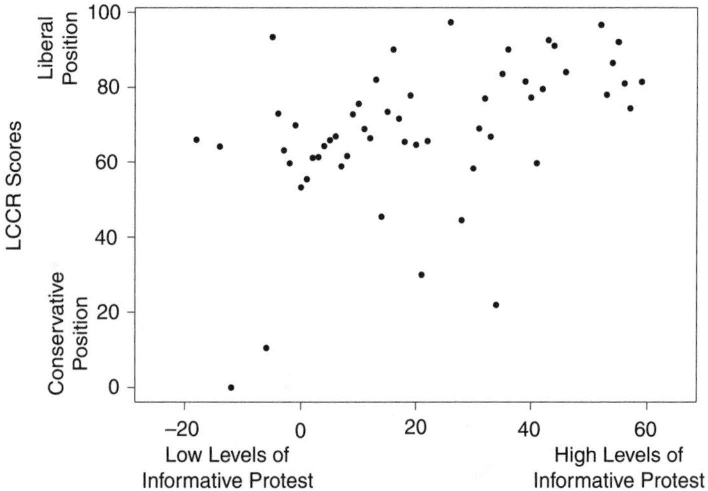

FIGURE 3.3. Congressional LCCR scores and minority protest along an information continuum.

protest that occurred in each district, and the *y*-axis is the corresponding LCCR score. The scattered points do not refer to a specific representative, but rather to the average LCCR score of multiple legislators who witnessed the same number of minority protest actions in their districts. Representatives whose districts did not experience any minority protest actions, for example, had an average LCCR score of 52, while those whose districts witnessed a –12 continuum score, indicating a predominance of anti-minority protest events, averaged a very conservative LCCR score of 0. The trend is positive and increasing, indicating that higher levels of pro-minority protest in a district are related to more liberal roll-call votes on racial and ethnic issues. Representatives in districts where protest was especially prevalent, with a continuum score of 50, averaged a high liberal LCCR score of 75.

The previous two figures indicate that individual legislators respond to the cues contained in minority protest. Even greater support for this notion is provided when we examine the autoregressive distributed lagged models in Table 3.2. The first column in this table examines minority votes based on ideal point positions, the second minority votes based on LCCR scores, and the third examines every vote that was taken in a congressional session to create a liberal ideal point position. For each column, I control for the number of minorities in Congress, minority population, length of service, party affiliation, incumbency status, and public opinion. Though not presented in this table, I also include fixed effects for both the congressional session and the congressional district.[8] The final data consist of the voting behavior for each House congressional district over fourteen different congressional sessions.[9]

The results suggest several explanations for individual representatives' voting behavior on minority policies. The most significant explanatory variable is the party ideology of a representative. Democrats were significantly more likely than Republicans to support liberal policies for minorities. This result is not surprising, but nor was it expected. Southern Democrats

[8] Caution was taken in including fixed effects for each congressional district. While an F-test indicated that fixed effects should be included in the model, I also ran separate regressions without the fixed effects. The reason for this is that variables that seldom changed will have a hard time reaching statistical significance with a large number of fixed effects (Beck and Katz 2001). For my case, fixed effects could potentially underestimate the impact of a representative being an incumbent or even of the political party of the representative. The fixed-effects model did not change the majority of results. The measure of interest, minority protest, remained substantively and statistically significant.

[9] This characterization, which comprises repeated observations of the same unit, is time-series-cross-section (TSCS) data. Estimating TSCS data with an ordinary least squares (OLS) is likely to provide varying levels of confidence in our results for different ranges of minority protest continuum scores, as well as across different years in which protests occurred, also known as heteroskedasticity and contemporaneous correlation within the standard error (Beck and Katz 2004). As recommended by Beck and Katz (1995), I address this problem by first calculating the coefficients with OLS and then calculating panel-correct standard errors (PCSEs), which provide a better measure of the sampling variability of the OLS estimates. A requirement for using PCSE is a sufficient number of time intervals. While the number of time intervals in this study ($T = 14$ congressional sessions) is not large, nor is it tiny. Beck and Katz suggests results with more than ten intervals could be misleading. However, the simulated results of Beck and Katz (1995) reveal that PCSEs are very accurate when $T > 15$. As a precaution, I also estimated the results with more traditional approaches to dealing with TSCS, such as a GLS AR(1) model (Stimson 1985), and the substantive results remained unchanged.

were some of the most ardent critics of civil rights legislation in the 1960s, and it seemed likely that the differing views on race of northern and southern Democrats would render this variable insignificant. The coefficient likely benefits from the inclusion of a "South" dummy variable, however, which is in the expected direction but struggles to reach statistical significance.

The first two models in Table 3.2, those for ideal point positions and LCCR scores, offer the same conclusions in terms of understanding the influence of informative minority protest within a district. Therefore, I focus on the more complete and accurate ideal point estimates, which allow the reader to better understand the influential power of citizens' actions. Table 3.2 shows that representatives are responsive to the political environment in their districts. The variable of interest, minority protest, is positive and statistically significant. This result contrasts to the findings of the previous section, which used national-level protest to understand congressional behavior. The district-level cues reflect a direct link between citizens' political preferences and congressional leaders' votes. The occurrence of one minority protest event is unlikely to have any influence on government behavior; the coefficient is small for a one-unit change (an additional minority protest only makes a representative 0.09 percent more liberal). But as the information provided through citizens' protest behavior accumulates, so does the impact it has on Congress.

Substantively, a politician who sees fifty minority protests over the course of two years in his or her congressional district, as was the case for Representative John Pilcher (D-GA; Minority Ideal Point Position Score = 91 percent) in the Eighty-Seventh Congress, will be 5 percent more likely to vote in the liberal direction on minority issues when compared to others in this Congress. On the other hand, congressional leaders who witness few minority protest events in their districts, as was the case for House Representatives W. G. "Bill" Hefner (D-NC; Minority Ideal Point Position Score = 55.8 percent) and Richard Ichord (D-MO; Minority Ideal Point Position Score = 19 percent) in the Ninety-Fifth and

TABLE 3.2. *Factors that influence individual roll-call votes on minority issues*

	Minority Policies (Ideal Points) (1960–1995)	Minority Policies (LCCR) (1972–1995)	All Policies (Ideal Points) (1960–1995)
Lagged Dependent Variable	.25510*** 0.01036	0.09809*** (0.01341)	.02209*** (0.00639)
Minority Protest in $District_t$	.09810*** (0.00951)	0.13423* (0.06494)	0.00002 (0.00019)
Minority Protest in $District_{t-1}$	−0.03623 (0.02359)	0.12031 (0.06752)	−0.00025 (0.00017)
National Public $Opinion_t$	8.5700*** (1.1480)	0.55831 (1.70404)	−0.0742*** (0.00853)
National Public $Opinion_t$	0.7329*** (0.1175)	0.14011 (1.07184)	0.00004 (0.000875)
Black $Representative_t$	13.670*** (2.1990)	5.81664 (3.68895)	0.1590*** (0.01977)
Latino $Representative_t$	3.2110 (2.6390)	−0.12208 (4.40406)	0.12750*** (0.0261)
Democratic $Party_t$	30.480*** (0.7991)	40.21735*** (1.29007)	0.3787*** (0.00675)
Length of $Service_t$	−0.1788*** (0.02948)	−0.02395*** (0.04861)	−0.00051* (0.00024)
Percent of $Democrats_t$	5.0090** (1.8390)	−8.27324** (0.01949)	0.01649 (0.0155)
Southern $Districts_t$	−6.8700 (6.6750)	−19.97501* (9.52650)	−0.03261 (0.05708)
$Incumbent_t$	−6.5840*** (0.7597)	−1.83103 (1.18406)	0.03705*** (0.00620)
Minority Population in $District_t$	3.4080** (1.2810)	−0.39895 (2.03223)	0.02378 0.01566
Black Population in $District_t$	−4.6780** (1.5680)	2.51347 (2.52996)	0.00415* (0.01762)
N	9061	5411	7329
R^2	0.5329	0.6386	0.7994
adj. R^2	0.5165	0.6034	0.785

Notes: Statistical Significance is denoted as follows: significant at $^*p < .05$; $^{**}p < .01$; $^{***}p < .001$.

Ninety-First Congresses, respectively, will make decisions on minority issues that are unaffected by protest. In the most informative environments, when minority protest approaches a continuum score of 100, as Representative Frank Annuzio (D-IL; Minority Ideal Point Position Score = 98.4 percent) witnessed in his district during the Eighty-Ninth Congress, legislators are predicted to become nearly 10 percent more liberal on minority issues than others in Congress due to the social context of protest. These results reveal the influence that minority protest has on congressional leaders when the focus shifts to the district level.

There is also a role for national perspectives in this district-level narrative. When the country feels that race is an important problem facing the nation, representatives become more likely to take liberal positions on minority issues. In the first column in Table 3.2, I include the nation's feelings on race, which I refer to as public opinion, only as a control to assess whether these national attitudes render district-level political behavior insignificant. The result shows that these two variables are not competing with one another and that minority political protest exercises influence over the roll-call votes of representatives independent of national public opinion. Representatives do not ignore events that occur in their districts, but rather they consider these informative protest actions within a national framework.

Minority protest does not have an overarching influence on liberal policies more generally. While liberal votes on minority issues are a subset of all liberal votes taken, my theoretical framework suggests that minority protest would have a lesser impact on liberal policies than minority policies. The reason for this is that politicians consider specific social and political events relating to the issues on which they are voting. Minority protest would provide more information to representatives on a vote dealing with discrimination than on a war-related policy issue, for example. The last column in Table 3.2 supports this notion, and the coefficient on minority protest is insignificant. Politicians did not use the policy preferences voiced in minority protest as a general indication of how they ought to approach all liberal policies. Rather, the information expressed in minority protest specifically informed them of the importance of minority concerns.

Informative Protest, Political Parties, and Race

Thus far, we have seen that the average congressional representative was responsive to racial and ethnic minority political protest in his or her own district. But it would be naive to assume that congressional leaders make decisions based solely upon the behavior of their constituents. Their daily activities are likely to be constrained by some of the institutional norms that exist in the legislative branch, as well as by their unique individual characteristics. One of the most dominant institutional influences on congressional behavior is political parties, which provide politicians with a platform of coherent issue positions. Though there was much division in the Democratic Party in the early 1960s, mainly in the South, this party emerged from the civil rights era as a unified front in support of minority concerns. As a consequence, a vast majority of African Americans, Latinos, and even Asian Americans have voted heavily Democratic, and minorities now comprise the party's permanent base. Thus, it is unsurprising that Table 3.2 shows Democratic representatives to be more liberal on minority issues. One question worth considering is whether protest activities addressing racial issues were more informative and influential to Democratic politicians.

While the average congressional leader is likely to respond to political protest, Democratic representatives are twice as likely to be attentive to these political cues. Figure 3.4 shows how the voting behavior of Democrats and Republicans changed as the information in protest changed. When political activity simmers at low levels, it makes little difference to the liberality of a politician's vote. Over a two-year congressional session, however, Republican congressional leaders were likely to become at least 4 percent more liberal than other members

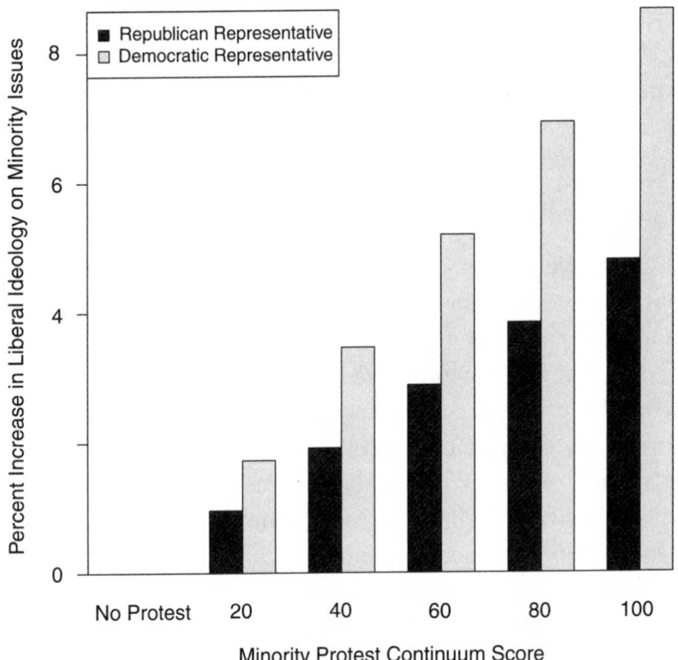

FIGURE 3.4. Democrat and Republican response to minority protest.

in the House of Representatives when they experienced minority protest with a continuum score of 100. Democrats, on the other hand, became 8 percent more liberal on minority issues when they experienced the same level of protest behavior.

Given the impact of political parties, we might also expect congressional representatives' race to mediate how receptive they are to minority political protest. Some studies have found that a representative's racial background dictates his or her support for minority issues (Canon 1999; Whitby 2002; Baker and Cook 2005). If we refer back to Table 3.2, there is support for this claim, at least for black representatives.[10] But race not only plays a role in terms of the politician who is making laws, it also plays a role in terms of the demographic makeup of the district a congressional leader represents.

[10] Latino Representatives are not more likely to offer liberal votes on minority issues. However, if we expand the examination to consider every bill voted on in Congress, we find Latinos more likely to vote liberal on multiple topics.

In 1982, amendments to the Voting Rights Act (VRA) ushered in a new method of creating descriptive representation through majority-minority districts, where the majority of citizens are racial and ethnic minorities. Redistricting and demographic shifts have affected a substantial growth in majority-minority districts over time. In 1980, there were twenty-seven majority-minority districts, but this number had more than doubled to fifty-six by 1992. The creation of majority-minority districts facilitates the election of minority representatives to office.[11] Irrespective of whether a minority is elected to office, moreover, the literature on Congress has suggested that the increase in the minority population is highly associated with representatives' (black or white) casting more liberal votes.

Does race, either through the individual characteristics of a representative or the demographic makeup of a district, facilitate the response to information in minority protest? In Table 3.3, I consider party, a representative's race, and the racial makeup of the district. Black representatives who belong to the Democratic Party and who reside in a majority-minority district are more receptive to information stemming from protest behavior than white Democrats who govern a district with a similar makeup. Black representatives in these districts are roughly 17 percent more likely than other members in the House of Representatives to cast a liberal vote on minority issues. Similarly situated white representatives are only 3 percent more likely to vote liberally on minority issues. Minority representatives are not always receptive to political activism, however. When African Americans represent districts where the racial minority does not constitute the demographic majority, they are less responsive to informative minority protest.

These results suggest an intriguing point that deserves further attention. There is a common notion that congressional representatives who are elected from heavily populated majority-minority districts do all that they can to address minority

[11] In addition, constituency preferences are equally likely to affect legislators' voting decisions from majority-minority districts as they are the roll-call votes cast by representatives in majority white districts (Gay 2007).

TABLE 3.3. *Responses of democratic representatives by race in majority-minority districts*

		Change in Ideology		Differences (%)
		Min Continuum Score (%)	Max Continuum Score (%)	
Black Democratic Representative	MMD	0.29	17.4	17.1
	Non-MMD	−0.052	−3	−2.9
White Democratic Representative	MMD	0.06	3.6	3.5
	Non-MMD	0.002		0.12

issues, regardless of whether protest actions are occurring in their districts. This simply is not true. It matters greatly whether minorities simply live in their district or are actively engaged in political protest in the district. In addition, both party affiliation and race affect the degree to which political protest informs politicians: Democrats and black members of Congress are more likely than their counterparts to be influenced. Thus, we may conclude that although black representatives and/or Democratic members of Congress might come into office with the goal of addressing racial issues, citizens' activism strengthens their resolve to do more, as was the case for Maxine Waters.

Conclusion

We have now come full circle back to the LA riots. These political protest events galvanized the nation, costing millions in damage, seeding doubts about the quality of our police forces and the judicial system, and inspiring national dialogue on race relations. To some in the media, these political protests were pointless and void of any valuable information that could improve the political and social conditions of minorities in South-Central California. But rather than scold her constituents for their behavior, Representative Maxine Waters sought to understand the roots of their discontent. In her eyes, the protest activities that followed the Rodney King ruling were more than a response to yet another perceived judicial injustice. They were the overflowing frustrations of citizens whose concerns about minority unemployment and inner-city issues had been ignored. These political actions were informative to Waters. Namely, the social environment of political protest, which encompassed hundreds of individuals engaging in contentious behavior, drew Representative Waters's attention to important issues in her district. Once aware of the gravity of her constituents' interests, she drew on the message in these actions, which emanated largely from one side of the issue space, when she introduced new bills, voted on policy issues, and interacted with other federal institutions.

There is nothing unique about Maxine Waters's response to the Rodney King events. As this chapter shows, representatives in Congress seek to understand the issues that affect their constituents. Congressional representatives do not come to Washington with this information in hand. No politician has the prior experience to be prepared to address all of the multiple issues that may arise in his or her district. Thus, they learn on the job and adapt to the changing political and social conditions of their congressional districts.

This chapter began with a simple inquiry into *whether* informative minority political actions were influential, but the true question that should be posed is, *how* are minority political actions informative? National minority political behavior is rarely, if ever, able to change aggregate decisions made by Congress. The relationship is more nuanced. To understand minority concerns voiced through political behavior, congressional leaders turn to their backyards. Politicians look at the content of minority protest actions that lie within their district. As the institution closest to the people, Congress is indeed influenced by citizens' grievances. When congressional representatives witnessed the scope of minority protests, which can be captured by the information continuum, they began to take more liberal positions on racial issues.

4

Knocking on the President's Door

The Impact of Minority Protest on Presidential Responsiveness

> *No effort to list the president's opportunities to use the prestige of his office to further civil rights could be adequate; from fireside chats to appearances at major events, the list is endless. All that is needed at the outset is a firm resolve to make the presidency a weapon for this democratic objective; the opportunities would then arise by themselves.*
>
> – *Dr. Martin Luther King Jr.*

Since the early twentieth century, racial and ethnic minorities have descended upon the South Lawn gates of the White House and at Lafayette Park in massive numbers, hoping to garner the president's attention. Such appeals have not been restricted to Washington; protesters throughout the nation have made appeals directly to the president. This chapter attempts to assess whether the information in these protest actions was able to resonate in the Oval Office and elicit a presidential response.

We saw in Chapter 3 that congressional representatives often look to informative protest actions within their own districts to understand and address citizens' concerns. When we shift our focus to the presidential branch of government, the scale of representation expands to include the entire nation, but the pursuit to understand the most pressing issues of citizens remains. As we shall see, the social context of minority protest has provided presidents with an understanding of racial and ethnic minority concerns.

Yet the president's relationship with minority protest is not characterized by whether he recognizes the social context of political protest, but rather by how he responds to the changing political atmosphere. Unlike the other two branches of government, the executive acts as an individual. The president is held solely responsible for the rhetoric and public policies that stem from the Oval Office. The position also carries a great deal of power and authority that sets the presidency apart from other governmental positions or institutions. As the opening quotation from Martin Luther King illustrates, it is this authority and power that civil rights leaders attempted to channel through their informative political actions. The response they received varied, reflecting the complexities of the Oval Office, the changing attitudes of mass public perceptions, and the individual beliefs of presidents. Accordingly, our analytic lens expands in this chapter from focusing on one form of presidential action to capture the multifarious forms of presidential responsiveness to minority protest, including presidential statements, press conferences, memoranda, executive orders, and even personal letters written by the president.

The chapter begins by discussing the benefits that presidents receive when they use protest as a resource for information. The next section offers a short historical overview of the relationship between presidential actions on race and protest behavior. This serves to highlight the presence of minority protest as a backdrop for many influential presidential policies that addressed minority concerns. These historical snippets are followed by a more systematic examination of the various forms of presidential behavior and rhetoric through an analysis of the *Public Papers of the Presidents*. This systematic assessment presents evidence that minority political protest guides presidents to respond in a public forum, as opposed to addressing race through more private actions. I conclude with some thoughts on how the varying views of presidential responsiveness really offer the same story of protest influence.

How Presidents Use the Information in Protest

Theodore Sorsensen (2005) refers to the presidential agenda as being an open book, one that can be altered by changing political environments. It is difficult to imagine a president succeeding in policymaking who tried to follow a rigorous outline of policy implementation over his four years in office. Such an approach would illustrate his lack of flexibility, and flexibility is an essential quality of presidential leadership. The power of the president lies in his ability to address crises or important issues facing the nation, to move with the shifting waves of international and domestic problems as they arise (Pious 1979).

Thus, presidential leadership requires adapting to current events. Most importantly, the president must draw on existing sources of information to cater to the needs of the American public. If the president wants to help himself, he must, in the words of Richard Neustadt, "reach out as widely as he can for every scrap of fact, opinion, gossip, bearing on his interests in relationships as President" (1991, 129). These scholarly words have often been confirmed by executive actions. President Nixon stated that in order to get a sense of the national mood, "You take Gallup's polls ... on what is the number one issue.... Don't ever assume that what you think is the big issue is going to be the big issue tomorrow. I constantly have to tell my staff, 'Keep checking, checking with Congressmen, Senators, but also with people generally in the country.'" It is this constant pursuit of information that allows protest activity to become yet another window for the president to understand citizens' preferences.

The information in minority protest serves as a shortcut that helps the president to make decisions. Similar to congressional leaders, the president is learning on the job. With every issue, there arises a unique set of problems that must be addressed. One issue that awaits every president is racial concerns. Certainly in the era of the modern presidency, and arguably from the foundation of the United States, every president has had to wrestle with the best approach to handling racial and ethnic minority concerns (Ashmore 1994). Changing perceptions of race require the president to become informed about how this issue is evolving. There is probably no better source for understanding that which ails the racial and ethnic minority community than for the individuals in that community to express their problems. Though mass opinion has been helpful in guiding the president's actions on race (see Cohen 1997, 88–89), the general public is not always aware of the intricate details of minority grievances or what the right policies may be to address these concerns. Moreover, as Chapter 2 revealed, the public's perception of the importance of minority concerns is in large part informed by the social context of minority protest. The president is also observing this information. And if we assume that other presidents strive to learn in ways similar to those Nixon described, we may conclude that presidential administrations are substantially more active than the American public in becoming informed about race.

But recognizing there are informative cues in political protest is one thing; responding to these cues is another. Presidents may witness protest events that are large, well-organized, contentious, and primarily emanating from pro-minority voices but remain neutral toward or unresponsive to the concerns these events express. Being unresponsive may itself be considered an action (Bachrach and Baratz 1962), an approach that several presidents have taken to issues of race. It has been suggested that presidential inaction itself offers the American public a cue on the views the president considers acceptable (Rich 2007, 233). But modern presidents have not practiced this sort of "benign neglect" for the entire course of their tenures in office.[1] Each has implemented race-related policies,

[1] This is a term used by Daniel Moynihan in a 1970 White House memo under Nixon's Administration. Yet even in this administration, policies and programs such as the Minority Business Enterprise were implemented.

offered commentary on minority concerns, and engaged with the minority community to try to solve problems.

Presidential attention to race has been shaped in part by minority activism, which functions as the proverbial carrot and stick. In terms of the carrot, there are incentives for the president to acknowledge or act on the information embedded in protest. He can benefit from policy initiatives advanced to address the issues voiced in minority protest. He can use protest actions to gauge the salience of topics (Geer 1996). Understanding the importance of an issue can allow the president to determine the best course of response. Finally, the competing sides of protest afford the president the ability to take, and even retake, the right stance on an issue. These are all positive aspects of information that stem from political protests.

But there is also the proverbial stick: ignoring the information contained in protest can have negative political consequences. Left unaddressed, minority protest actions can shape public opinion and make it seem the president is avoiding a critical topic, lowering his approval ratings (Edwards et al., 1995). The president also runs the risk of alienating a minority voting bloc when he refuses to cater to the policies voiced in protest actions. Though this may be a greater consequence for Democratic presidents, Republican presidents also make appeals in the hope of obtaining minority votes (Ashmore 1997). Thus, the information in protest can improve the president's policies, but it also acts as a warning of potential problems that may lie ahead for his administration. These are helpful insights into racial issues that the president has often heeded.

Snippets of History: The President's Race-Related Policies and Political Protest

It may seem inconceivable that a few individuals could direct the attention of a political official whose job is to govern millions. After all, thousands of protest actions occur each year to which the president remains unresponsive. Yet when we assess former presidents' actions on race, we find that citizens' political protest behavior has often preceded the implementation of executive policies.

In the historical overview that follows, we see that every president since Kennedy has been confronted with and responded to informative political protest. The character of presidential responses and the reasoning behind these responses has varied, but in each case, minority protest seems to have helped the president shape his policies on race – and in some cases even defined it.

Kennedy and Civil Rights

President John F. Kennedy can be understood as being timid on race relations (Riley 1999, 237). But Kennedy's legacy on race – the initiation of policies that would lead to the 1964 Civil Rights Act – showed a strong commitment to improving racial and ethnic minority conditions. Many of Kennedy's major policy innovations and executive actions came in response to political behavior. Protest events surrounding James Meredith, the first African American to attend the University of Mississippi, led to President Kennedy directly interacting with Governor Ross Barnett of Mississippi to facilitate Meredith's admission. As an extension of Kennedy's administration, Attorney General Robert F. Kennedy also placed a telephone call to Governor Barnett to lobby on Meredith's behalf.[2] Protest actions surrounding the freedom rides were followed by President Kennedy's action to enforce the *Boynton v. Virginia* Supreme Court decision that prohibited segregation of interstate travel.[3] And the events in Birmingham in 1963 informed President Kennedy that he could no longer put off implementing his New Frontier program.

[2] Richard Reeves, *President Kennedy: Profile of Power* (Simon and Schuster, 1994) 358–360.

[3] Ibid., 127–30.

Lyndon Johnson and Civil Rights

President Lyndon B. Johnson's approach to race was a continuation and heightening of the efforts Kennedy started. And similar to Kennedy, President Johnson was aware of the informative signals found in political protest and used these events to further extend his policy agenda on racial issues. The events in Selma during Bloody Sunday are illustrative of Johnson's resolve. Led by a strong coalition and including six hundred civilians, the Selma protesters attempted to cross the Edmund Pettus Bridge, where they were met by state and local law enforcement agents who used batons and tear gas against them. In responding to the protest events, Johnson stated, "I am certain Americans everywhere join in deploring the brutality with which a number of Negro citizens of Alabama were treated when they sought to dramatize their deep and sincere interest in attaining the precious right to vote. The best legal talent in the Federal Government is engaged in preparing legislation which will secure that right for every American."[4] The events in Selma lasted for three weeks, but the information they conveyed on the importance of addressing race and voting would linger on. Later that year, President Johnson issued an executive order that directed the attorney general to provide assistance to federal agencies in enforcing Title VI of the Civil Rights Act of 1964 and recommended legislation that would lead to the Voting Rights Act of 1965.[5]

Richard Nixon and the Chicano Movement

Presidential responsiveness to political protest continued in the post–civil rights era. Nixon's approach to race was an economic one. He aimed to increase "black capitalism," primarily by establishing the Office of Minority Business in the Commerce Department. During his time in office, he also expanded the

[4] Lyndon B Johnson, "Statement by the President on the Situation in Selma, Alabama," March 9, 1965, *Public Papers of the President*, 104.

[5] President Johnson issued Executive Order 11247 and later spoke about his actions in a message addressed to Congress on February 10, 1966.

government's understanding of minority issues to be inclusive of Hispanics. In 1970, for the first time, the Census collected data on Spanish-speaking and Spanish-surname Americans. Nixon also began to convey Hispanic concerns in his speeches and opened a genuine dialogue about their well-being. In his first year in office, he set the agenda by stating, "Many members of this significant minority group have been too long denied genuine, equal opportunity. For example, many have been denied the dignity that comes from useful job training, good jobs, and a real share in American enterprise."[6]

Events that occurred in the Chicano movement highlight the attention Nixon paid to protest. On August 29, 1970, one of the largest-ever protests for Mexican rights occurred in Los Angeles, California. The event, referred to as the National Chicano Moratorium demonstrations, was designed to voice concerns over the disproportionate number of casualties suffered by young Mexican Americans in the Vietnam War (Escobar 1993, 1483). It became perhaps the most contentious event in Mexican Americans' struggle for equal opportunity. When the protest was over, forty had been injured, and three were dead. Rubén Salazar, an esteemed journalist who often reported on important issues affecting Mexican Americans, was among the dead. His death galvanized the Latino community as a whole (Escobar 1993), and the protest and its outcome sparked greater public awareness of racial and ethnic concerns. The next year, 1971, President Nixon recognized the informative cues from protest actions by acknowledging in his State of the Union that "For the ... Mexican-American, and for those others in our land who have not had an equal chance, the Nation at last has begun to confront the need to press open the door of full and equal opportunity, and of human dignity."[7] This was the first time

[6] Richard Nixon, "Statement on Signing the Bill Establishing the Cabinet Committee on Opportunities for Spanish-Speaking People." December 21, 1969. *Public Papers of the Presidents.*

[7] Richard Nixon, "Annual Message to the Congress on the State of the Union." January 22, 1971. *Public Papers of the Presidents*, 26.

in the modern presidency that a president directly mentioned Mexican Americans and addressed their struggle for equality in a State of the Union address.

Jimmy Carter and the Black College Day March

President Jimmy Carter did not hesitate to discuss minority problems and to use executive orders to address race relations. Through these orders, he created an advisory committee on small and minority business ownership to steer subcontracts toward minority firms (Executive Order 12190). Carter made changes to the FCC by increasing the flow of federal advertising dollars to stations owned by racial and ethnic minorities.[8] He also submitted an amicus brief in favor of affirmative action in *Regents of the University of California v. Bakke*, a case that reviewed the role of race-based preferential treatment in the academic admissions process. President Carter did not gain much political capital with civil rights activists through these actions, however; activists tended to view them as an "awkward attempt to support affirmative action while condemning quotas" (O'Reilly 1995, 345).

One of the Carter administration's most significant legacies on minority policies came in response to political protest from historically black colleges and universities (HBCUs). These protests emerged on college campuses in 1980, when the federal government was considering cutting funding for HBCUs. The U.S. Department of Education wanted to integrate black colleges with a greater number of white students, merging state-funded black colleges into the larger state education systems. Many in the black community, however, viewed this as an infringement upon the prerogatives of HBCUs and a threat to their preservation.

On September 29, 1980, minority students descended upon Washington to protest the Department of Education's

[8] Jimmy Carter, "Telecommunications Minority Assistance Program Announcement of Administration Program." January 31, 1978. *Public Papers of the Presidents.*

plan. The events of this day had several characteristics that made presidential attention to them unavoidable. Reports of the U.S. Capitol police suggest roughly eight thousand individuals attended, and DC police officers suggested the number could have been over twenty thousand.[9] The march had strong organizational support from many universities and civil rights organizations, and it culminated a string of smaller protests that had previously occurred on the campuses of southern universities.

The organizer of the event was Tony Brown, a former dean of communications at Howard University who produced his own TV show. Brown indicated the project had been in preparation for months. In the weeks leading up to the protest event, he projected that half a million people would attend on September 29, a date selected because it coincided with the Congressional Black Caucus Legislative Weekend and the National Association of Black Journalists convention. [10]

President Carter wanted to act before the protests were in full swing, hoping to potentially head off any negative attention. Thus, after isolated college protests had occurred, and just weeks before the march on Washington was scheduled to take place, he issued Executive Order 12232 on August 8, 1980, which strengthened and expanded the capacity of historically black colleges.[11] After the Black College Day March took place, while signing into law the Education Amendments of 1980, Carter stated, "We've put more Federal resources behind the historically black colleges, which award nearly half the degrees received by black students in our country.... The legislation I'm signing today reflects the diversity and adds to the strength of American higher education. It helps parents

[9] Thomas Morgan, "A Sense of Commitment and Festivity Marks First Black College Day March," *Washington Post*, September 30, 1980.

[10] He indicated this in an interview with *Jet* Magazine on September 11, 1980.

[11] This executive order directed the secretary of education to implement a federal initiative to increase HBCU participation in federally funded programs. It also directed the secretary of education to establish annual goals with the heads of each executive agency as an oversight measure to ensure that HBCUs were being fairly represented in federally funded programs.

and students pay college costs. It strengthens our research universities. It strengthens our black colleges."[12]

Ronald Reagan and Anti-Apartheid Protests

In stark contrast to President Carter, President Reagan pushed for states' rights. He believed that federal government should not overreach to infringe upon the practices of local businesses and private firms. This philosophy drove both his economic and his social policies. When this rationale was applied to race relations, it led him to oppose certain policies that could have benefited the minority community. He vetoed a bill expanding civil rights legislation, for example, because it opened the door to "excessive government regulation."[13] On the whole, the Reagan administration has been described as creating a "counterrevolution" on race-related policies (Ashmore 1995, 297). Often-cited examples include his reluctance to extend the Voting Rights Act, allowing tax breaks for educational institutions that still engaged in segregation, and his criticism of the welfare state. Scholars have suggested that Reagan's anti-minority rights position spilled over into his response to political activism. The main example given of the president's reluctance is his unwillingness to be persuaded by the anti-apartheid movement.

The anti-apartheid movement shifted racial and ethnic minority protest actions from domestic issues toward the international woes of South Africa, where blacks lived in a government-instituted racial hierarchy that privileged white South Africans. For racial and ethnic minorities living in the United States, the situation in South Africa was reminiscent of the similar inequality struggle that had occurred in the American system. As a consequence in part, at least, of such reflections, various political protests in 1984 asked the U.S.

[12] Jimmy Carter, "Sterling, Virginia Remarks on Signing the Education Amendments of 1980 Into Law." October 3, 1980. *Public Papers of the Presidents.*

[13] Stated on March 25, 1988 in a Question and Answer session with the Members of the Center for the Study of the Presidency.

government to send a signal of disapproval to South Africa with condemning statements and economic sanctions. On April 4, 1985, four thousand marchers appeared in front of the South African embassy in Washington, DC, asking the government to act. The protest in DC was one tentacle of a larger movement occurring in the nation. Protests actions began taking place on college campus throughout the country, where students were pressuring their universities to discontinue any investments with firms conducting business in South Africa.

The combined social context indicated that these protest actions were sufficiently informative to exercise a strong influence. The movement had support from civil rights organizations, the Congressional Black Caucus, local politicians, esteemed professors, and celebrities. It lasted over an extended period of time and involved thousands of individuals. It was contentious, involving police presence at multiple events and a number of arrests – one arrest in particular involved Amy Carter, former president Jimmy Carter's daughter. The voices against apartheid also dominated the issue space for this topic.

A cursory reading of historical accounts might lead one to believe that President Reagan was unresponsive to the information in these protest events. This perception is only buttressed by the president's actions on September 25, 1986, when he vetoed a congressional bill that would have instituted comprehensive sanctions against South Africa. This narrative, however, is far too critical of the president's response to protest behavior. Mere months after the major protest event in April, President Reagan used executive orders to place sanctions on South Africa. Executive Order 12532 prohibited the making or approval of bank loans to the South African government and the extension of export marketing support to U.S. firms employing South Africans that did not adhere to fair-labor standards. In addition, the executive order called for an increase in the amount of funding provided for scholarships in South Africa to victims of apartheid. Later that year, on October 1, Executive Order 12535 prohibited the importation of the South African Krugerrand (South African gold coins) into the United States. These policies were directly in line with the request of minority protesters that the U.S. government place economic restrictions on South Africa.

Thus, Reagan's decision to veto the congressional bill cannot serve as the only measure for understanding whether he was receptive to the salient information in political protests. Actually, in the eyes of President Reagan, passing the Congressional bill that established sanctions would have been yet another concession among the many he had already made. In particular, he saw his issuance of Executive Order 12532 as having already partially addressed the issue of sanctions. Thus, the question is not whether President Reagan was responsive to political activism. He was, and his response was supportive of positions laid out in protest actions. The question, rather, should be whether he went far enough in championing the protesters' concerns. It is apparent, in any case, that political protest drew attention to an important topic that led to favorable presidential response.

George H. W. Bush and the LA Riots

President George H. W. Bush's legacy in terms of his attention to race is controversial. He actively tried to reform the welfare system, arguing that welfare made individuals dependent on the government. He led a strong assault against racial quotas and anything resembling them. And he vetoed the Civil Rights Bill in 1990, making him the only president to veto a civil rights bill.[14] These executive policies did not sit well with blacks and Latinos, and they have been perceived as actively going against minority interests (O'Reilly 1995).

Yet in the midst of these controversial actions, President Bush also took positions favorable to racial and ethnic minorities on several occasions. One noteworthy stance came in the aftermath of the 1992 Rodney King uprisings in LA. After the

[14] Though he did later sign the very similar 1991 Civil Rights Act.

riots had dissipated, the information voiced in these protest actions did not fall on deaf ears. Standing in the midst of where the protest actions had taken place a week earlier and speaking at a Boys' and Girls' Club center, President Bush proclaimed, "Things aren't right in too many cities across our country, and we must not return to the status quo.... in the wake of the LA riots, in the wake of the lost generation of inner cities' lives, can any one of us argue that we have solved the problems of poverty and racism... ? And the answer is clearly no." His response was similar to that of congressional representative Maxine Waters, who we saw in Chapter 3 was motivated to act by these events, in that he touched on the economic conditions of South Central.

In the same speech, Bush implemented a strong executive policy by announcing a $19-million "Weed and Seed" program for the city of Los Angeles. The weeding aspect would attempt to rid the city of drug dealers, and the seeding component would provide financial resources to neighborhoods for improved educational facilities, employment opportunities, and social services. This program, as acknowledged by Bush, was a direct response to protest behavior.

William Clinton and the Million Man March

Sometimes referred to as the first black president, President Clinton was beloved by racial and ethnic minorities during his time in office. He averaged an 81 percent approval rating among blacks during his time in office and close to 90 percent in the last three years of his presidency.[15] It was not simply that he could play the saxophone in a way that reminded individuals of the sultry music from Motown, that he was viewed as a regular guy for appearing on Arsenio Hall's show, or that he was applauded for embracing black babies when he was on the campaign stump. These superficial attributes added to his allure, but black voters were more strongly drawn to his verbal commitment to addressing minority issues.

15 This statistic is drawn from a report released by Gallup (Newport 2010).

President Clinton was a strong advocate for minorities, primarily through his commentary. His rhetoric was constantly about recognizing race as an important topic. Clinton made discussing race a fixture in his speech. One phrase he used particularly often was "getting over the racial divide": Clinton used this phrase or a version of it in ninety-eight different speeches during his time in office. He also expanded his discussion of race to involve the American people. In his second term, Clinton implemented "One America in the Twenty-First Century: The Presidents' Race Initiative," a national forum to discuss racial issues. A commission was assembled to issue a report on the state of racial affairs – the first such commission since the Kerner Commission in 1968 under President Johnson. President Clinton stressed that the initiative was one he brought to the forefront on its own merits, not a reaction to the social climate. During the launch of the initiative, he stated that the plan was to be implemented "now, when there is more cause for hope than fear, when we are not driven to it by some emergency or social cataclysm."

That President Clinton led on many policies and initiatives that addressed racial and ethnic minority concerns, however, did not preclude him from responding and adapting his rhetoric in response to political protest. In 1995, after hundreds of thousands gathered on Capitol Hill for the Million Man March, Clinton took the opportunity to signal that he recognized the message being voiced in this protest action: "I honor the presence of hundreds of thousands of men in Washington today, committed to atonement and to personal responsibility, and the commitment of millions of other men and women who are African Americans to this cause."

The march may also have had a lingering impact, reinforcing and propelling the administration's view on race. One component of the Million Man March stressed the need for black men to make a stronger commitment to improve upon their efforts to reshape the state of black communities. President Clinton altered his rhetoric to encompass this message, stating, "Black men must also do their part and take renewed responsibility to address a generation of deepening social problems that disproportionately impact black Americans." This became a part of a larger message from the administration that both sides, black and white, needed to recognize their shortcomings and improve upon them to overcome the racial divide – a principle voiced throughout Clinton's term and was folded over into his race initiative.

Benefits and Limitations of the Historical Approach

This short overview has offered historical snippets around the subject of when presidents from Kennedy through Clinton took political action on minority policies. By no means is it an all-encompassing historical account. What is enlightening about this overview, however, is that it shows that on many occasions when the president addressed race, informative protest actions lurked in the background, potentially or definitively shaping the president's response. Yet there have also been times when protest did not prompt presidential action, which suggests that the overview may not be representative of the influence of political activism. Moreover, what qualifies as a response? Wilbur Rich (2007, 232) has written that some of these responses are racial acknowledgement gestures – mainly symbolic actions that are individual or event-specific but do not lead to any substantive change in black lives. Other responses clearly ushered in substantial change. This implies that some responses from the president are stronger than others. In the next section, I explore the various types of responses a president can make and attempt to quantify these reactions so that I may expand my theory to encompass a larger number of cases.

The Various Ways a President Can Respond

The role of the president is complicated and multifaceted, and it involves interacting with interest groups, congressional leaders, governors, judges, and the public as a whole. The president can be outgoing and open about his political intentions, or he can work in an insular fashion, keeping the public in the dark about his ideas and plans. The mix of private and public actions encompassed in the office affords the president various avenues through which to address racial and ethnic minority concerns.

It would be impossible to comprehensively classify the full scope of executive action, but I attempt a facsimile by considering six ways the president can respond to citizens' behavior: through presidential memoranda, public statements, press conferences, presidential letters, executive orders, and State of the Union addresses.[16] I further separate the response of the president into private actions (presidential memoranda and letters) and public actions (statements, press conferences, executive orders, and State of the Union addresses). Analysis of each mode of response offers unique insight into how presidents react to political cues from citizens' behavior.[17]

In terms of private actions, presidential letters are among the best sources of information for revealing personal relationships or offering insight into closed-door discussions. Presidents send letters for various reasons, ranging from addressing a public situation to expressing condolences for the death of a popular public figure. Presidential letters can be especially insightful into issues of race, because they provide

[16] This approach is similar to that of Edwards and Wood (1999), who suggest that scholars ought to examine multiple modes of presidential responsiveness. Naturally, there are other ways to measure presidential responsiveness that are not used in this study. For example, Canes-Wrone (2004) examines presidential responsiveness in terms of policy congruence, in which congruence is measured by whether or not the president's budgetary proposal on a given issue is the direction preferred by the mass public.

[17] Presidential memoranda and personal letters are considered "private" in a limited sense: these are forms of communication that are not directed toward the mass public. Moreover, there are a number of memoranda and letters that are not published in the *Public Papers of the Presidents*. For those memoranda and letters that are published by the office of the Federal Register, many are released after the referencing event has occurred. Thus, presidents often do not draft these documents with the intention of communicating with the American people. All public statements, press conferences, executive orders, and State of the Union addresses, however, are means by which the president directly engages with the public.

information about private interactions the president might not publicly acknowledge. President Eisenhower, for example, rarely discussed the consequence of the Supreme Court decision to integrate the public school system in a public forum. In a letter sent to Governor LeRoy Collins on March 31, 1956, however, Eisenhower addressed the governor's proposition to meet with the attorneys general. He wrote:

> Your telegram of March twenty-second, in which you suggest that a conference of Southern Governors and Attorneys General be called by me to review "the South's present problems in the whole field of racial relations," has had my thoughtful attention.... I am deeply cognizant of the difficult adjustments confronting some localities in complying with the school decision of the Supreme Court. It seems to me, however, that the progress already made in certain regions of the South before and since this decision is a clear indication that we can look forward to even greater progress if we can look to moderate and responsible leadership supported by a spirit of patience on the part of all of our people.

This letter suggests Eisenhower took a moderate pro-minority position on the question of segregation – a position he did not make public but that he shared with key members of government in writing.

The memorandum is also an effective mode of private presidential responsiveness. A memorandum is a pronouncement by the president issued to one of the federal agencies that either conveys information on an issue or directs a course of action. It is more than just a simple letter or note. Phillip Cooper states that "as a practical matter, the memorandum is being used as the equivalent of an executive order but without fitting into its existing legal requirements" (Cooper 2002, 83). Throughout the modern presidency, presidents have used memoranda to direct federal agencies in the administration of racial and ethnic issues. Richard Nixon, for example, sent a memorandum to the heads of all federal departments directing them to make "every reasonable effort to ensure that the Federal Government is an equal opportunity employer" (Woolley 2008). Likewise, Gerald Ford sent a memorandum to all federal agencies stressing the importance of his minority business development program. As these examples show, the presidential memorandum is a good measure of responsiveness that lacks the publicity of a public statement but at times carries the power of an executive order.

While private presidential actions are informative, the nation is less likely to be attentive to them than to public actions, which are made known to citizens through the press and the media. Probably the most publically visible form of presidential responsiveness is the public statement – which is not even a mode of action, strictly understood. Presidential public statements include all of the speeches, addresses, and signing statements of the president. They reveal the immediate response that presidents have to a particular protest event or cluster of protest events, and they often indicate how the president plans to address a set of grievances. Signing statements, on the other hand, reveal how presidents interpret a given bill or how they plan to implement legislation. The variety of statements a president can make is extensive, ranging from Lyndon Johnson's remarks on the anniversary of the creation of the League of United Latin American Citizens to George H. W. Bush's signing statement on the Civil Rights Act of 1991.

The press conference is a second form of public rhetoric that indicates a president's intentions. The press conference can be understood as a forum for presidential agenda-setting. As examined in this study, the "press conference" refers only to the remarks made by the president before the press corps submits questions. Thus, when the president makes remarks in this venue, he is not responding to a reporter's prompt but rather offering prepared comments that address a current situation.

While press conferences can be viewed as a venue for presidential rhetoric, similar to public statements, the regular interaction with the press makes this a venue where news is routinely disseminated to the public. It is less a response to a particular event or grouping of events than a place to keep the public informed about the actions of the administration. An example of a relevant press conference is the one Jimmy Carter held on January 17, 1979, in which he discussed the administration's plan to address the economic needs of disadvantaged minority groups.

Executive orders and the annual State of the Union Address are more formal public avenues for a president to address racial and ethnic minority concerns. The State of the Union address is typically given at the beginning of a year. During the address, the president puts forth his legislative proposals for the upcoming year and discusses major issues that are currently affecting the nation. While State of the Union addresses are not political actions like executive orders, they reveal much about how the president responds to citizens' political behavior. The State of the Union address allows presidents to be strategic in their actions (Cohen 1995; Ostrom and Simon 1988). Presidential speeches allow the president not only to react to national events but also to manipulate these events (Simon and Ostrom 1985).

Executive orders, finally, showcase the president's independence, because they are policies that do not require the approval of Congress to be invoked. In addition, Congress rarely challenges these orders. Moe and Howell (1999), looking at roughly a twenty-five-year time period (1973–1997) that included approximately a thousand executive orders, found that executive orders from the president have only been challenged thirty-seven times by Congress. Out of the thirty-seven challenges, only three were successfully overturned. The extremely low percentage of challenges suggests the formidable power of the executive to act unilaterally through the executive order.

Not only is the executive order a powerful resource for the president, but executive orders that deal with issues of race and ethnicity have become more common in the modern presidency. Executive orders addressing racial or ethnic minority issues moved to prominence in the early 1940s with Franklin Roosevelt's establishment of the Fair Employment Practice Commission in 1943. After Roosevelt, Harry Truman issued an executive order that desegregated the military. Dwight Eisenhower worked to integrate schools through an executive order that provided assistance for the removal of an obstruction of justice within the state of Arkansas. John F. Kennedy issued similar orders for the state of Alabama. Lyndon Johnson, probably the most notable crusader for minorities via executive orders, issued executive orders that allowed for equal employment in federal hiring. Some argue that the establishment of affirmative action in federal employment did not arise from the Civil Rights Act of 1964, but rather stemmed from executive orders that President Johnson issued (King and Ragsdale 1988). Jimmy Carter issued various orders that facilitated the entrance of immigrants and refugees into the United States. And even Richard Nixon, who some might argue hindered minority opportunities (Bonastia 2000), issued an executive order to coordinate a national program for minority business enterprises.

Since executive orders, memoranda, public statements, press conferences, presidential letters, and State of the Union addresses reveal a considerable amount of autonomy in the president's decisions, it is likely that individual characteristics will be reflected in these forms of presidential action. Moreover, because these forms of executive behavior are autonomous, both sole credit and blame can be discerned from presidents' behavior. Hence, these public and private responses are approaches the president can use to respond to minority concerns.

Presidential Reaction to Informative Minority Protest

The previous section leaves little doubt that there are many ways to determine how the president can address race. An informational source that can be helpful in examining these different modes of attention is the volumes of the *Public Papers of the Presidents* series published by the Office of the Federal Register.[18] The Federal Register keeps an impressive record

[18] This series is accessible in electronic form through the *American Presidency Data Project* (Woolley and Peters 2008). All information in this section was generated using this data source.

of the president's daily actions and the speeches he delivers. It also keeps record of certain personal letters and internal memoranda. To assess presidential attention to race, I conducted content analysis on the *Public Papers of the Presidents* produced from 1960 through 1995. Given the enormity of such information, I used a wide range of keywords to retrieve material pertaining to racial and ethnic issues; these keywords are listed in the appendix.[19] Each entry returned from the keyword search was read for its content to ensure its relevance to minority concerns. If at any time in an executive order, memorandum, press conference, presidential letter, or presidential statement the president addressed a racial or ethnic concern, this document was coded with a 1; otherwise, the document was coded with a 0. By treating presidents' attention to race in this fashion, we can move toward a more systematic way of understanding executive actions on race-related issues. Moreover, the analysis can provide a comparable measure across presidents.

Figure 4.1 lays out presidential attention to race across all the presidents in the period under consideration.[20] This figure is more insightful than the historical review I offered in the beginning of the chapter. It illustrates that there have been major surges in the number of occasions when the president addressed racial and ethnic minority concerns. The era of the civil rights movement saw arguably the greatest attention to race-related policies, primarily under Lyndon B. Johnson. There was a major decline in this attention when President Nixon came into office in the late 1960s, but then there was

[19] A few of the words that were used to search for pertinent content include: discrimination, immigration, education of underprivileged students, welfare programs, and assistance for low-income families. Expanding minority issues beyond civil rights is an important aspect of this analysis. Minorities not only marched for issues of civil rights but they also protested on issues of poverty, as seen by the Poor People's March and Demonstration in May and June of 1968 (Mars 1969). Nick Kotz writes that even the great leaders during the heart of the civil rights movement believed "that the problems of civil rights and poverty were inextricably connected" (Kotz 2005, 300).

[20] The occasions the President addressed race are summed together by quarter.

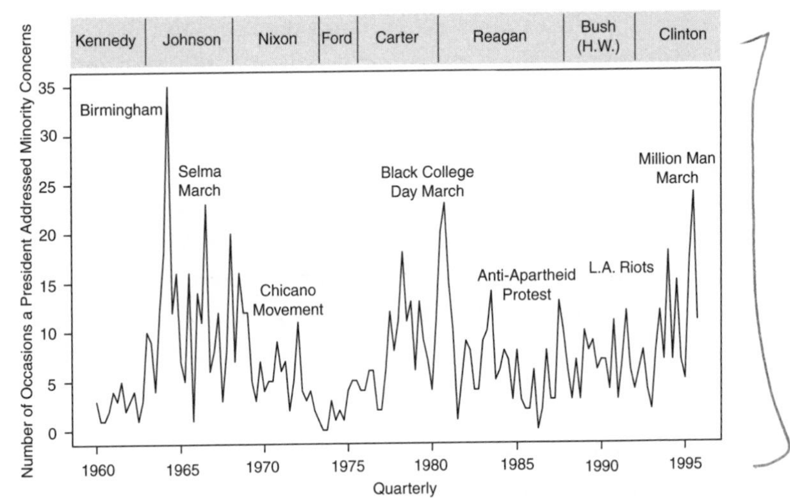

FIGURE 4.1. Presidents' attention to race-related policies, 1960–1995.

a resurgence under Carter's administration. In the 1980s, Presidents Ronald Reagan and George H. W. Bush addressed minority concerns on fewer occasions. Yet in the 1990s, with the arrival of President Clinton, the executive office was once again focusing more attention on minority policies.

The major spikes in the number of occasions on which the president addressed race were often preceded by minority protest events. Examining only the events I covered in the historical snippet accounts for some of the larger surges. It is interesting to note that the events in Birmingham, the Black College Day March, and the Million Man March are all associated with a large increase in the occasions the president addressed race. Coincidentally, these protests occurred when a Democrat held the presidential office. Events such as the Chicano movement, anti-apartheid protest, and the LA riots prompted less of a response and occurred when a Republican president led the nation. Regardless of political party, however, the table confirms that minority protest was occurring in the background at times when the president attempted to take a stronger stance on minority issues. We could take this conclusion a step further and suggest that protest behavior, at least in some cases, set the president's agenda on race relations.

While Figure 4.1 is illuminating, it tracks only increases in presidential activity, not how presidents went about addressing minority concerns. In this figure, for example, public press conferences are treated as equivalent to personal letters. Similarly, memoranda or signing statements are not distinguished from executive orders or the State of the Union address. It may be that the president's attention to minority concerns tends to be expressed through particular avenues and not others. To offer more insight into the different presidential approaches to addressing race, I separate the modes of response into distinct categories in Table 4.1. In this table, the total number of documents in which the president responds to racial and ethnic concerns is aggregated by quarter. The State of the Union address is measured slightly differently from the other forms of presidential action. Since the president only offers the State of the Union address once per year, I measured presidential attention in this speech by the number of sentences regarding issues of race or ethnicity in a given year, checking the context of the speech to ensure that each sentence was pertinent to racial and ethnic minority concerns.[21]

It is evident that some presidents addressed racial and ethnic minority concerns more aggressively than others, though it is important to note that for some presidents I do not include information on their entire term. I only include one year's worth of information for President Eisenhower and three years' worth for President Clinton, both of whom served eight years in office. In addition, some presidents were simply in office for a longer period of time, potentially allowing them greater opportunities to take up minority concerns. These points notwithstanding, Table 4.1 clearly shows that presidents have taken different approaches in addressing issues of race. President Carter issued nearly twice as many executive

[21] The final number of sentences was also cross-referenced with information stemming from the *Policy Agenda Project*. This served as a robustness check to assure that potentially relevant sentences were not overlooked.

TABLE 4.1. *Frequency of responsiveness to racial and ethnic minority concerns by type of presidential action*

	Letters	Press	Statements	Memo.	SOU Address	Orders
Eisenhower (1960)	1	0	7	0	7	0
Kennedy (1961–1963)	9	10	36	2	23	9
Johnson (1963–1968)	13	17	189	3	67	8
Nixon (1969–1973)	6	1	78	4	32	5
Ford (1973–1976)	3	2	32	3	27	3
Carter (1977–1980)	4	8	138	7	76	17
Reagan (1981–1988)	3	3	46	2	66	8
Bush (1989–1992)	0	5	30	1	29	5
Clinton (1993–1995)	1	3	45	7	79	5

Notes: Data on presidential letters, press conferences, public statements, memoranda, and executive orders were compiled by the author using the Presidential Public Papers. Data on the State of the Union Address was compiled from the *Policy Agendas Project.*

Letter = Number of presidential letters

News Press = Number of press conferences

Statements = Number of occasions a public statement was made, including Signing Statements.

SOU Address = Number of sentences in the State of the Union Address Orders = Number of executive orders

orders (17) as any other president in this time period; however, President Clinton was more likely to address minority issues in his State of the Union address (79 sentences). Even the most conservative presidents, Nixon and Reagan, were attentive to the concerns of minorities – and in some cases offered more attention to minority issues than did their liberal counterparts. While all of the presidents addressed minority concerns, Lyndon B. Johnson's overall record appears to be the most impressive. Among the six forms of presidential action and rhetoric, Johnson has the highest levels of attention for three of the six categories. Incidentally, Chapter 2 showed that President Johnson's time in office coincided with the period when protest was at its most salient levels.

The layout of presidential attention to race in Table 4.1 overlaps with the discussion of presidential behavior earlier in this chapter. We can use regression techniques to establish an empirical link that offers greater verification of the relationship between incidents of presidential attention and minority protest actions. I believe informative minority protest behavior was at least partially responsible for driving presidential actions, but other factors may explain when the president decided to address minority concerns. For instance, a president's approval rating could restrict when he is able to focus on public preferences (Canes-Wrone and Schotts 2004). In addition, any effect that stems from minority political protest could be an artifact of the general political atmosphere of the civil rights movement. This would mean, in turn, that political protest is restricted in its influence on the president to this period of movement activity. To account for these possibilities, I include a measure of the president's approval rating and a dummy variable for the civil rights movement (1955–1968) into the regression model.

Because I am addressing minority issues during the modern presidency, differences in attention to minority issues could be a large function of a presidents' ideology. Since the 1960s, the Democratic Party has made a strong effort to make minority issues a major component of its party platform (Carmines and Stimson 1989). Some have argued that racial and ethnic minority issues have been the greatest factor in explaining the transformation of political parties during this period (Pomper 1989). Thus, Democratic presidents are likely to be more susceptible to public pressure from minorities, who ask them to uphold the positions taken in their party's platform.

Finally, institutional constraints of the executive office could further hinder the activities of the president. Divided government, in particular, can potentially limit the president's ability to act. In addition, an upcoming election has been shown to dictate presidents' behavior (Jacobs and Shapiro 2000, 42–44). To account for the effect of divided government, I include a dummy variable that indicates whether the president's party is in control of Congress. I also include a four-year dummy variable to signify election years. Accounting for these alternative explanations should provide a more nuanced understanding of presidential responsiveness to racial and ethnic minority concerns.

Tables 4.2 and 4.3 reveal the exact level of influence that informative minority protest actions had on the president's attention toward minority concerns in any given quarter. In particular, I want to focus on the immediate effect of minority activism expressed in the variable *Protest_t*. In terms of the two private modes of presidential behavior (Table 4.2), the information in political protest influenced only presidential letters. And though statistically significant, the increase is marginal. Given an annual average of thirty-six political protests, all of which have some social characteristic that increases their continuum score, minority behavior only led to two additional letters that addressed race during a president's four-year term.[22] The significance of this figure is further devalued when we consider the meager impact a presidential letter may have on the minority community. A more substantial private response would be the president's use of the memorandum, but here the impact is insignificant. Simply put, presidents do not use memoranda to respond to minority political protest. Instead of citizens' behavior influencing presidential memos, situations of divided government actually decreased the number of memos the president sent to other governmental agencies.

[22] The following calculation is used to reach this figure: 36 × .0034 × 16 = 1.96 *letters*. To arrive at this solution, I multiply the protest activities, 36, by the coefficient on protest, .0034, and the number of quarters in a four-year term, 16.

TABLE 4.2. *Private presidential responsiveness to minority issues, 1960–1995*

	Letters	Memoranda
(Intercept)	−0.5063	0.5773*
	(0.3473)	(0.3139)
Lagged Dependent	0.1236	−0.0639
	(0.0852)	(0.0859)
Minority Protest$_t$	0.0034*	−0.0006
	(0.0018)	(0.0016)
Minority Protest$_{t-1}$	0.0015	−0.0018
	(0.0021)	(0.0018)
Public Opinion$_t$	−0.0125	−0.0003
	(0.0125)	(0.0113)
Public Opinion$_{t-1}$	0.0298	−0.0072
	(0.0235)	(0.0212)
Democratic President	0.0422	−0.0519
	(0.1007)	(0.0911)
Divided Government$_t$	0.2777	−0.5992*
	(0.2479)	(0.2241)
Democratic Congress	0.4070	−0.2297
	(0.2559)	(0.2304)
Presidential Approval	0.0047	0.0038
	(0.0042)	(0.0037)
Civil Rights Movement	0.0735	−0.1295
	(0.1928)	(0.1741)
Protest$_{t-1}$:Public Opinion$_{t-1}$	−0.0003*	0.0001
	(0.0001)	(0.0001)
N	143	143
R^2	0.2444	0.1568
adj. R^2	0.1810	0.0860
Resid. sd	0.4969	0.4476

Notes: Statistical Significance is denoted as follows: significant at $^*p < .05$; $^{**}p < .01$; $^{***}p < .001$. The dependent variables, presidential letters and memorandum in a quarter, are private actions that are often unbeknown to the general public.

Was the influence of political protest greater when it was conducted during periods when public opinion held race to be an important topic? The interaction terms in Table 4.2 indicate that informative minority protest actions were not more likely to resonate with presidents during favorable periods of public opinion; in the case of letters, the probability actually decreased.

Whereas the influence of minority protest on the president's private actions was mixed, the president's public behavior reveals a different story. With the exception of the State of the Union address, minority protest did influence the attention paid by the president to minority concerns. First, the president's daily rhetoric was heightened by salient political behavior. During a four-year term, presidents offered, on average, twelve additional public statements that addressed race and two press conferences that discussed minority concerns when they witnessed the scope of minority protest expanding along an information continuum. These results suggest that protest makes the president more likely to broach the topic of race and proactively set the agenda for the press corps after being informed by citizens' behavior.

Though presidential rhetoric on minority issues does lend insight into a president's potential agenda, press conferences and public statements consist of words that offer the promise of action. An executive order, on the other hand, is a form of presidential legislation that signals an active response to citizens' political behavior. Table 4.3 shows that protest actions reflecting a minority grievance were successful in producing an executive order that addressed minority concerns.

The only public presidential response not associated with minority protest actions is the president's State of the Union Address. Minorities' political protest behavior and mass public opinion viewing race as the most important problem, when considered independently, are either insignificant or not in the expected direction in the State of the Union address model. Conversely, the interaction term is both statistically significant and in the expected direction. This indicates that when a larger portion of the American public shares the concerns voiced in minority political behavior, the president will respond in the largest political arena to demonstrate his dedication to minority issues.

The impact of informative political protest extends beyond the movement era of minority actions. Consider the influence of the civil rights movement; the general political atmosphere

TABLE 4.3. *Public presidential responsiveness to minority issues, 1960–1995*

	Press	Statements	Executive Orders	SOU Addresses
(Intercept)	−1.3441*	4.7747*	1.5373*	5.3779
	(0.4074)	(2.4348)	(0.5191)	(3.3361)
Lagged Dependent	−0.0784	0.2213*	0.0678	−0.0497
	(0.0831)	(0.0812)	(0.0844)	(0.1784)
Minority Protest$_t$	0.0035*	0.0078*	0.0142*	−0.0142*
	(0.0021)	(0.0125)	(0.0027)	(0.0075)
Minority Protest$_{t-1}$	−0.0022	0.0050	−0.0017	−0.0067
	(0.0024)	(0.0145)	(0.0030)	(0.0074)
Public Opinion$_t$	−0.0256*	0.0473	−0.0236	0.1408
	(0.0149)	(0.0870)	(0.0185)	(0.1041)
Public Opinion$_{t-1}$	0.0364	−0.0264	−0.0684*	0.0654
	(0.0277)	(0.1641)	(0.0352)	(0.1454)
 Democratic President	0.0018	2.1313*	0.1054	−0.2770
	(0.1178)	(0.7115)	(0.1482)	(1.1800)
Democratic Congress	1.0495*	1.1968	−0.2097	−2.0524 
	(0.3003)	(1.7801)	(0.3778)	(1.7267)
Divided Government	0.6540*	−2.6447	−0.6540*	−1.8664
	(0.2892)	(1.7286)	(0.3684)	(1.8190)
Presidential Approval	0.0131*	−0.0312	−0.0131*	0.0182
	(0.0049)	(0.0288)	(0.0061)	(0.0528)
Civil Rights Movement	0.0627	−1.5010	0.1037	−3.8746
	(0.2254)	(1.3575)	(0.2849)	(3.2057)
Protest$_{t-1}$:Public Opinion$_{t-1}$	−0.0001	−0.0003	0.0002	0.0011*
	(0.0002)	(0.0009)	(0.0002)	(0.0005)
N	143	143	143	35
R^2	0.3276	0.4357	0.1762	0.4216
adj. R^2	0.2711	0.3883	0.1070	0.1449
Resid. sd	0.5815	3.4502	0.7316	2.5761

Notes: Statistical Significance is denoted as follows: significant at $^*p < .05$; $^{**}p < .01$; $^{***}p < .001$. The dependent variables are public presidential actions. 'Press' is the number of news press conferences in which the president addressed minority issues in a quarter. 'Statements' represents the number of occasions a public statement was made relating to minority concerns, including signing statements, in a quarter. 'Executive Orders' is the number of orders made by the president in a given quarter. 'SOU Address' represents annual information on the number of sentences in the State of the Union Address that relates to racial and ethnic minority issues.

during this period of time is statistically insignificant. This result suggests that the gains of the civil rights movement did not occur simply because the movement took place, but rather because there was a deeper mechanism that brought about change. Even controlling for the influence of the movement in the State of the Union address model, the interaction of citizens' political protest behavior and public opinion still had an effect on presidential responsiveness.

We have observed a strong presidential response to minority protest through various modes of political action. But did presidents address minority concerns immediately, or did they allow some time to pass? The auto-distributed lagged models in Tables 4.2 and 4.3 provide an understanding of temporal changes. Through press conferences, public statements, and executive orders, the president responded to the information in minority political protest within a three-month time period, or equivalently, within the same quarter.[23] The cues from minority political behavior clearly helped presidents to govern, and they did so rapidly.

Conclusion

The results of this chapter afford a deeper understanding of the relationship between minority protest and presidential behavior. The literature has produced conflicting results regarding the influence of minority protest. Historical examinations of presidential action have suggested that presidents were responsive to protest activities (Button 1989; McAdam 1982; Riley 1999; O'Reilly 1995; Kotz 2005; Branch 1989; Branch 1999). Yet the results of an empirical study using statistical analysis conclude that the relationship is not statistically significant (Hill 1998). This chapter bridges the divide, offering credence to both sides of the debate. For historical examinations of minority protest and social movements, this

[23] This is indicated by the variable *Protest* at time period *t* being statistically significant, whereas Protest at time period *t* – 1 is insignificant.

chapter suggests that citizens' political actions did influence presidential attention to minority concerns. However, we should be careful not to overstate the impact of minority protest actions. For certain modes of presidential responsiveness, the political success of protest relies heavily on its ability to galvanize public perceptions. Moreover, the impact is limited in scope. It is on this point that empirical studies are partially correct. The influence of minority behavior is not all encompassing and is restricted primarily to the public domain.

This chapter also demonstrates that it is necessary to assess the various forms of responsiveness a president uses to address minority concerns. Naturally, analyzing six different presidential actions introduces an unavoidable question: which presidential behavior is most effective in dealing with the grievances expressed by racial and ethnic minorities? This is an important question that future research must address. However, it does seem clear that results that focus on one or even two forms of presidential action will likely offer a biased depiction of responsiveness.

Finally, these findings potentially portray the president as being a reactive leader on racial inequality. It is unlikely that President Lyndon B. Johnson knew, years in advance, that his administration would be an important force for defining race relations in this nation in a way that few have done before or that any have replicated since. More likely, he confidently addressed race because the political cues stemming from minority protest were most informative during his time in office. He responded to the information he received by implementing sweeping policy changes and adopting rhetoric sensitive to minority concerns. I do not mean to suggest that every policy issued by Lyndon B. Johnson (or any president for that matter) dealing with racial and ethnic minority concerns was a response to political protest. A conclusion of this sort would truly be misleading. This chapter's historical review and regression analyses demonstrate that a host of factors influence when and how the president addresses minority concerns. However, the information in political protest is among these factors. When the scope of minority protest behavior expanded to include political organizations, massive crowds, and contentious actions that lasted over time, it alerted presidents of an important issue. These protest actions were often in favor of minority rights, providing greater details on racial issues and offering presidents a coherent signal to favor minority policies. Presidents have used this continuum of information to shape their administrations.

5

Appealing to an Unlikely Branch

Minority Political Protest and the Supreme Court

> *We couldn't get anything through Congress... Nothing. We couldn't even get the anti-lynching bill through. So you had to go to the courts. That was the only place that was a possibility. And we go and look at that and say, "Good God, that ain't no chance either." And so some of us said, "Let's bang it in there and bang it in there, bang it in there, bang it in there." And now where you going now? You know you can go to the courts if you want to know where we is now. That's where we is now.*
>
> – *Thurgood Marshall, interview with Juan Williams, 1989*

Can the information stemming from minority protest garner a response from the Supreme Court? More specifically, does the Court respond to political behavior that expresses a racial or ethnic minority grievance? Justice Thurgood Marshall was at times indecisive about the answer to this question. When asked directly whether it was useless for minorities to appeal to the Supreme Court, he responded, "I can't say that, but you see what the record shows" (Williams 1998).[1] This response – neither confirming nor denying the possibility – reveals Justice Marshall's uncertainty about the effectiveness of minority appeals to the Supreme Court. He was even less

[1] This is drawn from a Thurgood Marshall interview with Juan Williams that occurred over several months in 1989 (Williams 1998).

certain whether these appeals for government action should be made in the form of political protest.[2]

Thurgood Marshall's life experiences positioned him as one of the few people who could offer insight into the relationship between political activism and judicial behavior. The first African American to serve on the Supreme Court, he was a scholar, lawyer, and American revolutionary. He also headed the legal defense team for the National Association for the Advancement of Colored People. Justice Marshall's background and achievements gave him a unique vantage point. Over his lifetime, he went from serving as a significant figure in the most influential organization of the civil rights movement to being an outspoken and dominant voice in one of the most sacred political institutions of our government.

Marshall's perceptions of the impact of political protest were far from optimistic. In his view, protest activities, especially those activities that broke the law, had little influence outside of the media coverage they received (Williams 1998, 343). Though later in his life he acknowledged that Martin Luther King had a profound influence on government (341), Justice Marshall nonetheless questioned whether protest behavior was the correct vehicle for change.

Scholars often echo Justice Marshall's uncertainty, but rarely do they empirically test this question. Works of history point to a strong correlation between minority movements and progressive achievements made under the Warren Court, as evidenced by such decisions as *Brown v. Board of Education* (1954), which desegregated schools; *Louisiana v. United States* (1965), which invalidated the use of the literacy test for voting; *Watson v. City of Memphis* (1965), which allowed for racial minorities to use public areas in Memphis; and *Edwards v. South Carolina* (1963), which asserted the

2 On several occasions he disputed with Martin Luther King Jr. on whether violent and unlawful protests activities were the best tactic to implement (Williams 1998, 343).

right to peaceable assembly.[3] Not only did race-related cases appear before the Court more frequently in this era of heightened protest, but racial and ethnic minorities received more favorable decisions from the Warren Court than from the Burger and Rehnquist Courts that followed (Ulmer and Thompson 1981; Baum 1988; Blasi 1983).[4]

Since *Brown v. Board of Education*, scholars have suggested a positive relationship between the Supreme Court and minority policy goals. The Court's progressivism has been understood as having been an inspiration to minority activism (Kluger 1976; Woodward 1976; Wasby et al. 1977; Pritchett 1964).[5] The Supreme Court has also been credited with establishing a favorable climate for the passage of civil rights legislation (Levin 1979, 80) and as an effective "cheerleader" for minority rights, winning adherents to its preferred policy (Canon 1992). The Court, in essence, may be considered an ally of minority political activism. If this is indeed the case, are protest activities influencing judicial behavior? And if so, what are the conditions that lead to a favorable response from this branch of federal government?

In this chapter, I extend the information continuum theory to consider the actions of the Supreme Court. As in Chapter 3 on Congress, I explore both the individual and aggregate decisions of the Court. Yet quite different from Congress, and even from the presidency, informative protest actions do not have the same currency with the Court, in that they do not directly influence the actions of justices. As we will see in this chapter, minority political protest

[3] The Warren Court witnessed a significant increase in the number of minority cases the Court heard. This was possibly a consequence of potential litigants' interpreting politically salient Court decisions as in indication of the Court's willingness to hear additional cases that addressed race (Baird 2004).

[4] The positive public opinion that blacks have of the Supreme Court is partially explained by the residual effects of the Warren Court (Caldeira and Gibson 1992, 1140).

[5] While this has stood as a long-held belief, more recent works argue that the Supreme Court did little to inspire the protest actions of racial and ethnic minorities (Rosenberg 1991; Klarman 2004, 377).

in and of itself has had little influence on the number of minority cases the Supreme Court decided to hear or the percentage of minority-favorable rulings rendered in these cases. Instead, the story is really one of interacting influences. When informative cues from minority protest were linked to public perceptions of race as an important national issue, the Supreme Court responded by increasing the number of race-related cases it decided to hear. Even though the aggregate Court has not been attentive to salient political protest behavior, individual justices are themselves attuned to political preferences expressed through minority protest actions. Even Justice Marshall, who already had a record of supporting liberal positions, offered a greater number of liberal votes in the face of favorable public opinion and informative political protest. Overall, this chapter demonstrates that the information in protest behavior does indeed find a way to resonate with the Supreme Court.

Information Continuum: Barriers and Benefits in the Judicial Setting

Barriers to Informative Minority Protest

At first glance, the Supreme Court would seem an unlikely institution to respond to minority protest behavior. Political protest takes place outside the walls of the courthouse, after all, and these external social appeals are in many ways at odds with the internal institutional norms and procedures of the court. Two leading theories of legal scholarship, the legal and attitudinal models, highlight the difficulty here. In the legal model view, the Court accepts and decides cases based upon the facts of the cases, rule of law, and legal principles (Kahn 1999; Gillman and Clayton 1999). The attitudinal model, by contrast, argues that justices' individual political preferences play a dominant role in their decision making (Segal and Spaeth 1993; 2002). Justices who harbor a more liberal ideology are more likely to make liberal decisions than conservative justices. The same is true of conservatives. Those on the bench with a conservative ideology are likely to take a conservative line on cases.[6]

The legal and attitudinal models of judicial behavior are insightful and focus on the institutional norms of the Supreme Court. They also offer alternate theoretical foundations that cast doubt on the influence of protest actions and exclude any consideration of extra-institutional events, suggesting either that justices are uninformed about national protest incidents or that they are unconcerned with them. By and large, the models do not consider that the justice who serves on the bench goes home at night to observe and experience the same social transformations that affect other Americans. Are justices not changed by these events? The attitudinal model allows for at least the possibility of this change: in it, justices' ideological preferences are not fixed. They are considered fluid, shifting from time to time (Baum 1988; Ulmer 1973; Ulmer and Thompson 1981). Yet justices' political preferences often do not fluctuate due to the passage of time, but rather in response to the catalyst of social change (Mishler and Sheehan, 1996, 175).[7] As Supreme Court Justice Cardozo admitted, "The great tides and currents which engulf the rest of men do not turn aside in their course and pass the judge by" (1921, 167–68).

Even if the Supreme Court is attentive to and influenced by societal conditions – which would suggest that justices are sensitive to the information contained in minority protest – minority interests expressed through political activism face another obstacle: they must compete with the majoritarian nature of the Court. Majoritarian theory tells us that the Supreme Court sacrifices racial and ethnic minority interests

[6] The relationship between ideology and voting behavior is a strong one, with a correlation of 78 percent since the Warren Court (Segal 2009, 28).

[7] Mishler and Sheehan (1996) view public opinion as the societal condition that shapes public perceptions. The argument they laid out added to a growing perception that citizens' opinion affects Supreme Court decisions (Flemming and Wood 1997; Funston 1975; Hurwitz et al. 2004; McGuire and Stimson 2004; Mishler and Sheehan 1993, 1996; Norpoth and Segal 1994).

in order to promote the popular preferences of the American public (Ely 1980; Spann 1993). Moreover, the formal safeguards of principled adjudication cannot be relied upon to ensure that judges will operate free of the influence of majoritarian preferences when they endeavor to address the interests of racial and ethnic minorities (Spann 1993, 25–26).

But just as it can coexist with judicial norms and procedures, the influence of political activism can work within the framework of a majoritarian notion of the Court. In the majoritarian conception, minority interests are understood to be separate from popular public opinion. Often in practice, however, minority interests, expressed through political protest, can shape majoritarian preferences and indirectly impact the Court. Indeed, this is true for issues of race. As we saw in Chapter 2, race relations came to the forefront of politics due in part to political activism. If justices indeed act as "black-robed *Homo sapiens*," a description offered by Sidney Ulmer (1970, 580) to describe justices' commonality with the average citizen, then race should be on the minds of individuals who serve on the bench. Moreover, the information in protest activities should shape justices' perceptions of race as this information also shifts public opinion. Thus, the barriers posed to minority activism by the nature of the court may be overcome by the signals through which political protest informs justices about the state of the world.

In essence, certain benefits of the information continuum make it appealing and helpful for justices to take notice of minority protest activity, whereas the institutional procedures and legal norms of the Court can create an environment that allows justices to recognize these benefits. I consider these points further in the section that follows.

Benefits of an Information Continuum

Many theories that explain executive and legislative behavior tend to promote elections as the driving force behind governmental action. Politicians want to keep their jobs, and the quickest way for them to become unemployed is to ignore the citizens who voted them into office. But the judicial branch does not operate under the electoral constraint. Holding lifelong tenure, Supreme Court justices are able to defend and take issue on unpopular minority grievances without the fear of being removed from office. The very same institutional procedures that allow justices to evade the repercussions of majoritarian votes offer a hopeful environment for minority preferences that have gone unaddressed. Without the constraining links to political parties, lobbying firms, and special-interest groups that beset other branches of government, the Court allows for equity and influence for citizens (McCann 1986, 118). This is the reason some have written that the Court is the most promising federal venue for citizens to seek a response to their political behavior. The Court is able to respond to social events when other institutions may hesitate to do so (Sax 1971, 51). Aryeh Neier (1982) notes that dating back to the 1950s, "the courts have been the most accessible and, often, the most effective instrument of government for bringing about changes in public policy sought by social protest movements" (9).

Neier's point is an astute one, but it does leave open the question *how* minority protest actions come to the attention of the Court. First, minority protest that is expansive in scope, meaning that it has strong organizational support, mass engagement by activists that persists over time, and a contentious environment, signals the importance of civil rights and civil liberties issues for racial and ethnic minority communities. This information can serve as an indispensible resource for the Supreme Court at the agenda-setting stage, at which the justices decide which cases to hear. Similar to presidents and congressional leaders, the Court does not address a fixed list of issues. It possesses discretionary jurisdiction: the justices select only a small number of cases from among the thousands filed for their consideration each term. The Court has used discretionary jurisdiction to disproportionately select cases in which the federal government is an involved party, those that cause dissension among lower-court judges, and cases involving civil liberties issues (see Tanenhaus et al. 1963; Ulmer et al. 1972). In its selection process, the Court also considers the importance of the issues at the heart of a case (Baum 2010, 91). This is where the seeds of influence for informative protest behavior begin to sprout. The social characteristics of protest behavior give rise to public attention and interest. They propel the status of issues from the subject of casual conversations in private discussions to unavoidable debates taking place on a national platform. In justices' attempt to assess the relevance of the issues at stake in the cases they select among, protest behavior serves as a social resource to determine importance.

Another way the protest information continuum can aid justices is by giving them a greater understanding of the specific issues involved in a case. As protest raises the profile of an issue, it also publicizes the grievances expressed in political activism. Justices are aware that their rulings will not only affect the two parties involved in a particular dispute but will also have widespread ramifications for peripheral groups that do not have direct legal representation in the case. These groups often express their views through amicus curiae briefs, which are unsolicited opinions offered to the Court, and through social and political activism. Social activism in the form of political protest allows the arguments of a case to extend beyond the confines of the courthouse walls. Whereas the president and Congress make use of the concerns voiced in protest behavior to shape policy, the Supreme Court can use these expressed concerns to obtain a deeper understanding of the grievances expressed by minority groups. These concerns are considered alongside additional briefs, political commentary, scholarly writings, census data reports, and many other forms of information that adds greater breadth of knowledge to the subject at hand. And indeed, it is clear that the Court relies on the voices of political commentary, media, and social conditions: in the *Regents of the University of California v. Bakke* (1978) case, for example, Supreme Court Justice Powell opened his opinion by acknowledging that the Court "needed all of this advice" stemming from social commentary to arrive at its decisions.[8]

The *Bakke* case is enlightening, because it demonstrates the interaction of protest with other social conditions, namely, mass public perceptions. *Bakke* involved a white male student who sued the Medical School of the University of California at Davis after he was denied admission despite having a GPA and standardized test scores superior to those of minorities who were admitted through an affirmative action program. The Supreme Court of California ruled that the Davis admissions program was unconstitutional, because it violated the equal protection clause of the Fourteenth Amendment.[9] The court also declared that any program that took race into consideration as an admissions criterion was unlawful.[10] This ruling gave support to those who contended that reverse discrimination had taken place in this situation, but the court's decision to exclude race from the admission process had a more profound implication. In essence, the court affirmed that the social and economic conditions in which racial and ethnic minority candidates are raised and educated do not unduly disadvantage them in the academic environment. Thus, the disproportionate social inequalities of racial background may not be accounted for or rectified by educational institutions.[11]

This implication was important enough to spark the attention of the Supreme Court, which led to its granting *certiorari*, expressing the Court's willingness to review the case. The oral arguments started in October of 1977. On October 4, sixteen hundred students assembled in Washington, DC, to march the

[8] Transcribed commentary

[9] *University of California Regents v. Bakke* 438 U.S. 265

[10] Ibid.

[11] Though many minorities were opposed to the lower-court ruling in *Bakke*, civil rights organizations opposed the decision of the Regents of the University of California to take the case to the Supreme Court, stating, "The circumstances surrounding the origin, development and conduct of this case show that it has not been presented in the true adversarial manner best suited for judicial resolution" (qtd. in Bell 1979).

two-mile stretch from the White House to the U.S. Capitol Building in protest against the possibility of a Supreme Court decision in the *Bakke* case that would end affirmative action.[12] The message voiced in these protest actions was a defense of affirmative action programs. Protesters indicated the benefits that previous affirmative action programs had provided and pointed out the inequality that remained, and would likely endure, if these programs were discontinued. In a raw assertion of discontent, one protester expressed her frustration by stating, "Minorities are still not free."[13] These words captured a message about inequality constantly voiced in the protests.

More protest actions would follow. DC councilmember Marion Berry said, "Today can't be the only day we protest. We must protest every day until *Bakke* is overturned."[14] Protest actions did not occur every day until the *Bakke* decision, but they were certainly frequent. By the time the Supreme Court rendered its decision in June 1978, the concerns of protesters had gained attention from the media and the mass public. In comparison to 1976, nearly twice as many people felt that race relations were the most important problem facing the nation in 1978, rising from 2 percent to 4 percent.[15] The issue of race would not again reach this level of prominence for another fourteen years.

The Court's decision that followed informative minority protest and strong public opinion was bittersweet for minority groups. The ruling moderated affirmative action. Allan Bakke was admitted to the University of California at Davis Medical School on the ground that the university's specific use

[12] *New York Times,* October 4, 1977.

[13] Joseph Whitaker, "1600 Students Protest Bakke Case," *Washington Post,* October 4, 1977.

[14] Ibid.

[15] As indicated in previous chapters, the Most Important Problem (MIP) questioned asked by Gallup is an open-ended question, meaning respondents can offer any answer they desire. This produces thousands of different answers when the questionnaire is fielded several times over the course of a year. Thus, for a topic to rise above 2–3 percent indicates a growing consensus that it is becoming an important issue.

of race in the admission process served as a quota system and thus was unconstitutional under the Fourteenth Amendment. However, all was not lost for protesters. The Supreme Court also recognized race as an important factor to consider in the admissions process – a factor that ought to continue to be considered alongside other important determinants for admission. In speaking to the *Washington Post* following the ruling, the U.S. Civil Rights Commission chairperson, Arthur Flemming, was optimistic about the decision, claiming that the Supreme Court had laid out a clear "mandate to proceed with affirmative action programs."[16]

The opinions of justices who favored affirmative action echoed some of the concerns voiced by protest activity. Protesters' main argument was that racial inequality was still rampant in the nation, and affirmative action programs were necessary to combat such inequalities. The justices who supported the University of California couched their defense in an argument that mirrored this discussion. Justice Brennan stated that societal opposition to change furthered inequality: "Massive official and private resistance prevented, and to a lesser extent still prevents, attainment of equal opportunity in education at all levels."[17] Justice Marshall's opinion highlighted the inequalities affecting racial minorities in more detail, noting that African Americans had an expected life span five years shorter than that of white Americans, an infant mortality rate twice as high, and a median income only 60 percent of that of white Americans. Furthermore, four times as many African Americans lived under the poverty line, black unemployment was double white unemployment, and the median income of college-educated black males was substantially lower than that of white males.[18]

The raw numbers produced by Justice Marshall revealed undeniable racial disparities, but the intensity of protest

[16] Harold Logan, "U.S. Rights Panel Backs Univ. Affirmative Action," *Washington Post*, July 2, 1978.
[17] *Regents of the University of California v. Bakke*, 438 U.S. 265 (1978).
[18] Ibid.

actions added further meaning to these statistics. The large number of protest activities that persisted throughout the trial indicated that the chasm between black and white achievement and prosperity remained unacceptable to many Americans. The harsh reality is that American society is unlikely to arrive at strict equality, where income, education, and social status are exactly equivalent for all racial groups. But achieving Justice Blackmun's hopeful goal of moving beyond "transitional inequality," when affirmative action programs are no longer needed, is obtainable. The indication that we have reached this point rests not in crossing a magical numerical bar but rather when the discontent with the status quo voiced by racial and ethnic minorities diminishes. The protest actions surrounding *Bakke* sent a clear message that as a society, the United States had not yet made it past the phase of "transitional inequality."

The *Bakke* case is only one example where protest occurred and a moderate degree of success followed. No justice came out and stated directly that his or her opinion rested on the backs of those voicing protest. But some of their views resembled those of protesters. In *Bakke*, as in the various events that surround presidential policies for racial and ethnic minorities, protest activity lurked in the background, providing an informative backdrop to the favorable judicial decision in the case. Notwithstanding this association, it may be difficult to demonstrate a relationship between informative protest and judicial behavior as expressed in Court opinions. After all, the opinion of the Court does not always inform us of individual justices' reasons for voting a certain way (Spaeth 1965, 879). However, justices' actions are undeniable. If we continue to see a trend of informative protest followed by favorable rulings, then this is strong evidence that the social context of citizens' political actions is signaling the Supreme Court of important issues, and the Court is using this information to shape its rulings. In the next section, I expand the discussion of informative protest to include multiple judicial actions on a series of minority cases.

Influencing Aggregate Decisions

There is much to gain by expanding our discussion to include multiple minority cases that the Supreme Court has ruled on over time. Such an expansion enables us to discern patterns of behavior and recognize trends. To examine these trends, we must first identify the policy stance of cases appearing before the Court. This may be difficult, since the legal basis for decisions normally disregards their applicability to public policy. Nevertheless, if cases are categorized according to the public policy to which they relate, then by extension it can be determined which cases relate to racial or ethnic minority groups. The U.S. Supreme Court Database (Spaeth 1999) accomplishes this goal by categorizing cases according to the various policy issues they affect. Consequently, I select all cases from Spaeth's (1999) precoded policy categories that relate to racial or ethnic minority issues from the time period 1960–1995.[19] Analyzing the total number of minority cases in a given year can be misleading, however. If the Court examines a large number of minority cases during a period in which many cases are being reviewed overall, the large number of cases might give the impression that the Court is more concerned with minority issues at that time than it is in a period in which the Court took fewer overall cases and a moderate number of minority cases.[20] Thus, I focus instead on the percentage of all cases the Supreme Court reviewed that dealt with racial or ethnic minority issues, as well as the percentage of these cases that received a favorable ruling.

[19] The categories that I consider racial or ethnic minority topics include the following: Voting Rights Act of 1965 (plus amendments), desegregation, affirmative action, reapportionment, poverty law (welfare benefits), immigration and naturalization, deportation, and sit-in demonstrations.

[20] To further this point, I would note that the Warren Court decided on fewer than 100 cases per year, whereas the later Burger Court decided on 153 cases in the 1972 term (Segal and Spaeth 1993, 186). Thus, twenty cases brought to the Warren Court on minority issues would signify proportionately greater attention to these issues than twenty cases brought to the Burger Court.

The abundance and depth of information found in the U.S. Supreme Court Database also allows for an analysis of the Court's disposition toward minority issues. All the cases considered in this study fall under the heading of civil rights claimants or civil liberties cases. Thereby, a favorable decision means that the Court is pro–civil rights or pro–civil liberties. For instance, if the Court reviews a case that deals with desegregation and is favorable toward the case, this means that the ruling was pro-desegregation. This same logic applies to pro-affirmative action, pro-welfare benefits, pro-voting rights, and so on. I establish a favorability measure for each justice, as well as for the entire Court, which is an average of the individual justices' scores for each case aggregated annually.

Figure 5.1 compares judicial behavior on minority cases with an information continuum of protest. The minority protest continuum score is the same metric for understanding the scope of protest activism used in previous chapters. This score is derived by first creating a unique score for each minority protest action based on the social characteristics of the protest event.[21] I then sum these protest scores over the entire year for pro-minority rights protests and anti-minority rights protest. The difference between these two values (anti-minority rights subtracted from pro-minority rights) is an aggregate protest continuum score, where positive values indicate prominent levels of protest activity that supported minority issues and negative values indicate significant levels of anti-minority rights protest that were opposed to these issues. While I allow

[21] Recall that the following social characteristics are used to capture the content of citizens' behavior: (1) protest activity that involves more than one hundred individuals, (2) protest activity that lasts more than a day, (3) protest activity that is supported by a political organization, (4) protest activity that results in property damage, (5) protest activity that garners a police presence, (6) protest activity that leads to an arrest, (7) protest activity that involves individuals carrying weapons, (8) protest activity that leads to injury, or (9) protest activity that involves death. I transform the nine definitions given above into binary variables and then sum across the binary variables to calculate a continuum score. Computed in this fashion, any given protest event can have a continuum score that ranges from zero to nine.

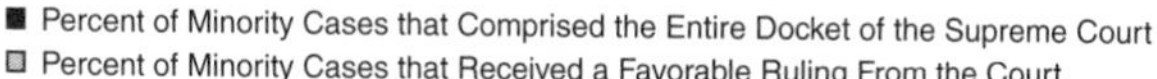

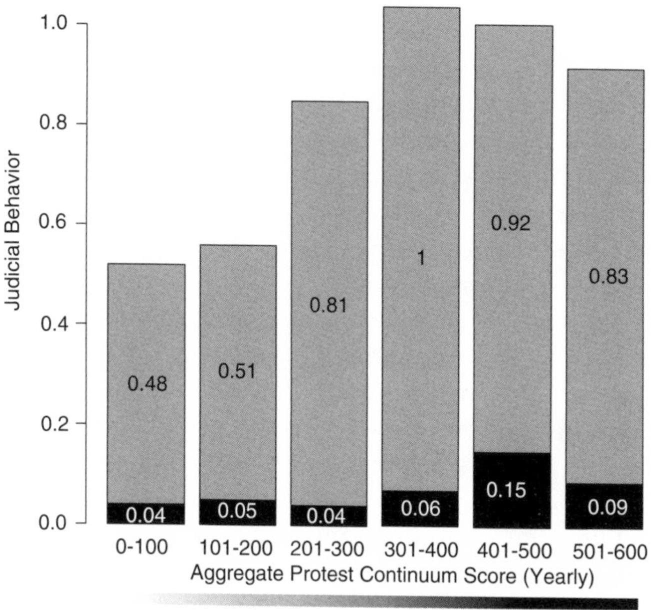

FIGURE 5.1. Protest and judicial behavior.

for both sides of the issue space to express protest concerns, pro-minority protest overshadows anti-minority protest in every year. Thus, the annual protest continuum scores are always positive and range from 0 to slightly over 600.

Based on Figure 5.1, informative protest actions correspond with judicial behavior. In this figure, the darker bars indicate the percentage of cases relating to minority issues that the Supreme Court decided to hear, and the lighter bars indicate the percentage of those minority cases that received a favorable ruling from the Court. During years when protest activities were less informative or lacked salient social characteristics such as organizational support, heavy citizen involvement, contentious behavior, and a clear indicator of whether pro-minority rights activities dominated the issue space, the

Supreme Court accepted fewer cases related to racial and ethnic minority concerns. When minority protest was the least informative, only 4 percent of the Supreme Court's docket involved race-related issues. For the years with a high minority protest continuum score, however, more than 9 percent of the Supreme Court docket involved cases that addressed race-related issues; nearly one in ten cases addressed minority issues. This is a strong association.

The relationship between protest activities and Supreme Court rulings is even more astonishing. In years in which minority protest was less informative (aggregate continuum scores below 300), the Court ruled favorably toward minorities only 48 percent of the time. Yet in years when the aggregate protest continuum score was between 301 and 400, every minority case received a favorable ruling; scores between 401 and 500 were associated with 92 percent of cases receiving a favorable ruling; and scores between 501 and 600 were associated with 83 percent of cases receiving a favorable ruling. On average, when the protest continuum score topped 300 in a given year, 90 percent of minority cases received a favorable ruling.

We can explore this relationship even further by assessing the trends of protest continuum scores and judicial behavior for each year. Figures 5.2 and 5.3 depict this relationship. In both figures, the dashed line indicates informative minority protest, and the solid dotted line illustrates judicial behavior. For ease of comparison, levels of informative minority protest are shown on the right-hand y-axis, and judicial behavior is shown on the left-hand y-axis. Figure 5.2 shows the annual percentage of minority cases that were granted *certiorari* overlapped with the associated minority protest continuum score. These two trends initially begin in opposite directions, but they converge within the first three years. By 1962, the Warren Court was walking nearly in lockstep with minority activism, deciding to review a greater percentage of minority cases than at any other period under consideration. Yet under the Burger Court (1969–1986), the pattern of minority behavior diverged drastically from the percentage of minority cases heard. There

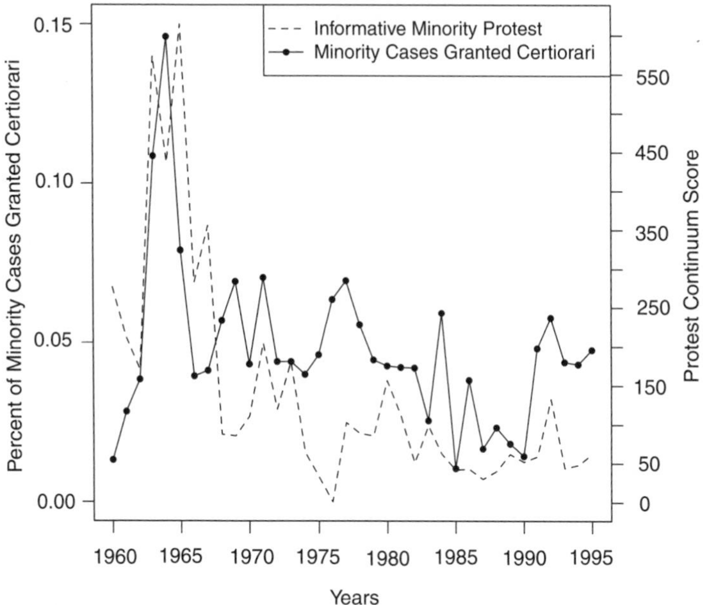

FIGURE 5.2. Informative minority protest and the percentage of minority cases taken by the Court.

is a considerable gap between the trends from 1974 through 1980. Also, the Court began to steadily decrease the number of minority cases it reviewed. To be fair, the Burger Court had little motivation to address issues of race. It witnessed the lowest level of informative minority protest in the period under study. There was a slightly greater overlap between the trends during the Rehnquist Court (1986–2005). In 1991 and 1992, on the heels of the Los Angeles riots, minority protest began to increase, and the percentage of minority cases heard by the Supreme Court also rose. The patterns of minority engagement and minority cases continued to mirror one another heading into the mid-1990s.

The relationship between minority protest and decisions rendered on minority cases is less significant, as Figure 5.3 shows. Yes, both trends reflect a steady decline from 1960 to 1995. And again, the Warren Court offered favorable decisions when minority protest occurred. But the vacillation in

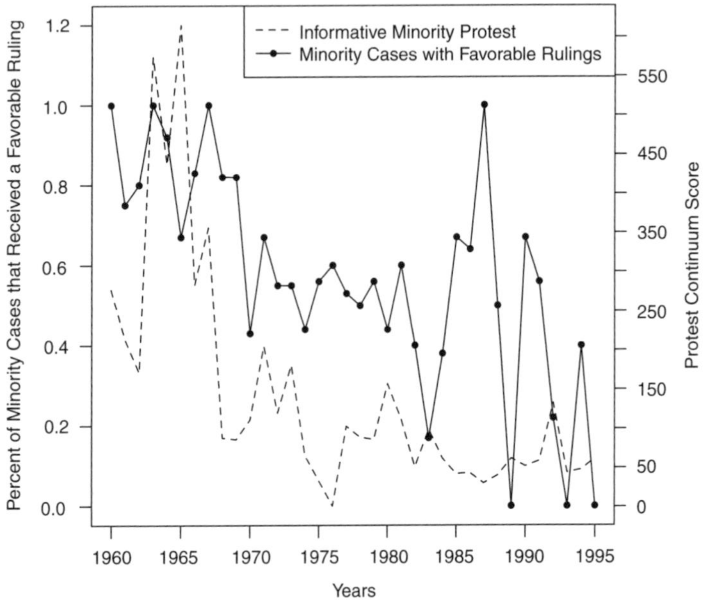

FIGURE 5.3. Informative minority protest and favorable rulings on minority cases.

the percentage of favorable rulings on minority cases during the Burger and Rehnquist courts appears unresponsive and unrelated to the information in minority protest. By 1983, this relationship was spurious at best.

The yearly examination of minority political actions in Figures 5.2 and 5.3 indicate a weaker relationship between informative political protest and judicial behavior than the aggregate associations presented in Figure 5.1. Yet taken collectively, these graphs hint that the Supreme Court did respond to political protest. How large was this response and what environments allowed the information in protest to resonate are questions that remain unanswered. To address these questions, I return to the autoregressive-distributed lagged model, a regression technique used in previous chapters to assess the influence of an information continuum.

The regression model offers the advantage of examining the influence of the information continuum theory alongside competing hypotheses. While justices may be responsive to the social context of political protest, there are likely to be other explanations for the Supreme Court's attention to minority concerns. Much discussion in the literature considers the ability of special-interest groups to influence the Supreme Court (Green 1994; Kluger 1976; Tushnet 1987; Klarman 2004), suggesting that minority interest groups make cases more likely to be reviewed and to receive a favorable decision. Special-interest groups can litigate the Court by providing detailed amicus curiae briefs to buttress the perspective of racial and ethnic minorities. Support from interest groups like the National Association for the Advancement of Colored People or the National Council of La Raza can further legitimize a protest issue in the eyes of the Court. Backing from such well-established groups may mark an issue as a nationally important topic that should garner the attention of justices. In order not to overstate the impact of my theoretical claims, I consider interest-group actions in the empirical model.

The actions of the solicitor general, the representative of the executive branch, can also influence the behavior of the Supreme Court. In particular, the solicitor general can influence the actions of the Court by submitting an amicus brief (Caplan 1987; Salokar 1992; Bailey et al. 2005; Segal 1988; Graham 2002, 2003). The work of Barbara Graham (2003) shows that the involvement of the solicitor general is among the strongest indicators of when the Supreme Court will attend to issues of civil rights. Though Graham's study does not include political protest, her findings suggest that the Department of Justice exercises a substantial degree of influence over the Court. Thus, I must consider the number of liberal amicus briefs that the solicitor general submits, which could increase the Court's attention to minority concerns.

Finally, a handful of other important factors may explain the Supreme Court's behavior toward minority issues. These include public mood (Stimson 1999) and the overall ideology of the Court (Mishler and Sheehan 1993). I account for these factors in the model. The public mood of the nation should not be confused with public opinion. Public mood is a three-to-five-year moving average detailing the liberal or conservative views of the nation, whereas public opinion, as I describe it here, focuses on national attitudes of race. More specifically, I measure public opinion as the percentage of individuals who consider issues of race to be the most important problem facing the nation in a given year. This variable is also interacted with informative minority protest.

The relationship among the various trends in Figures 5.1–5.3 – or lack thereof – may depend on the timing of the judicial process. It usually takes less than a year for the Supreme Court to review and decide upon a case. The time it takes a case to arrive at the Supreme Court, however, lengthens the overall process. If a case comes to the Supreme Court on appeal after the issue has been reviewed, this means that the issue has been examined by a lower court and has been in the public domain for a longer period of time. Consequently, a judicial response may be at least a year or two removed from the initial protest activities that expressed the concerns the case takes up.

This brings us to an interesting question: Is the Supreme Court responding to political behavior that took place just months before its ruling on a case, or is the Court reflecting on an enduring trend when justices offer their decisions? A short-term response from the Supreme Court would signal that this institution is attuned to the immediate concerns of minority interests, which would allow justices to use informative protest to assess cases they are currently considering. A long-term response from the Supreme Court, on the other hand, would indicate that a sustained political environment of informative protest exists over time, as indicated by a movement. In practice, both long-term movement-like behavior and spontaneous protest may influence the Court. Thus, I will assess the immediate and long-term impact of minority protest with the autoregressive-distributed lag model.

Examining the Court as a Unified Body

When the Supreme Court is examined as a unified body in Table 5.1, an interesting but complicated story emerges. The context of minority protest actions raised an important issue and aided the Court in recognizing the cases it should hear. The information in minority protest could only influence the Court, however, when a significant percentage of Americans felt that race was one of the most important problems facing the nation. Specifically, when less than 1 percent of the nation felt race was an important topic, informative minority protest did not lead to the Supreme Court increasing the number of minority cases it heard, but when race became more important in the public mind, the Court responded. The combination of an expanding scope of minority political protest, as captured by the information continuum, and mass public opinion viewing the issue of race as an important problem facing the nation partially drove the Supreme Court to also consider racial issues.

To offer a substantive example, compare the annual protest continuum score for minority protest actions that occurred in 1969 to that for 1992. While 133 informative minority protests occurred in 1992, 1969 only witnessed 89 informative minority protest events. Nevertheless, the events of 1969 had an influence on the Court nearly twice as great. The reason for this is that in 1992, on average, 5.2 percent of Americans felt that race was the most important topic on the national agenda, whereas an average of 11.7 percent felt this way in 1969.

The impact of political activism, aided by public perceptions, was not immediate. The results, presented in Table 5.1, indicate the Supreme Court reflected on the social conditions surrounding minority protest in the years that preceded its decisions about which cases to hear. The impact of minority protest combined with public opinion has lagged the actions of the Court by at least a year. During this period, minority protest provided an important avenue for the Court to

TABLE 5.1. *Influencing Supreme Court rulings and their decision to grant* certiorari *to minority cases*

	Minority Cases	Minority Rulings
(Intercept)	−3.6335	−48.9326
	(5.0375)	(97.1948)
Lagged Dependent	0.1291	0.3225
	(0.1370)	(0.2469)
Minority Protest$_t$	0.0063	−0.0934
	(0.0051)	(0.0897)
Minority Protests$_t$	−0.0045	−0.0007
	(0.0040)	(0.0744)
Public Opinion on Race$_t$	0.0771	−2.9920
	(0.0816)	(1.7549)
Public Opinion on Race^–*i*	−0.0535	−2.0579
	(0.1092)	(2.0173)
Court Ideology (Liberal)$_t$	0.1782	10.7177 *
	(0.2719)	(5.5790)
Amicus Curiae (Liberal)$_t$	0.0174	−0.5728
	(0.0214)	(0.4006)
Solicitor General*	0.8390 ***	8.0309
	(0.2406)	(5.0264)
Public Mood (Liberal)$_{t-4}$	0.0828	0.9242
	(0.0818)	(1.5667)
Civil Rights Movement$_t$	−2.9003	73.1968 *
	(2.0201)	(37.7456)
Protest$_{t-1}$:Public Opinion$_{t-1}$	0.0004*	0.0004
	(0.0002)	(0.0049)
N	32	32
R^2	0.8549	0.5574
adj. R^2	0.7751	0.3140
Resid. sd	1.1616	21.5895

Notes: Statistical Significance is denoted as follows: significant at $^*p < .05$; $^{**}p < .01$; $^{***}p < .001$. The dependent variable is the percentage of minority cases that were reviewed by the Supreme Court.

become aware of pertinent topics. The year 1963 is illustrative of this point as a time period in which both public opinion and political behavior combined in an unprecedented fashion. Political protests in this year were often led by strong political organizations, included large crowds of protesters, persisted over time, and frequently became contentious. Equally salient was public opinion, which reached beyond 50 percent of the nation expressing that race was a critical issue that must be addressed. The result of these two factors, as predicted by the regression output, was that at least 10 percent of all the cases the Court decided to hear in 1964 revolved around race. Justices were more attuned to the informational cues of minority protest when protest actions took place in environments of pronounced public opinion that advocated the importance of racial issues.

The interacting effect that minority protest and public opinion has on the Supreme Court holds up against competing theories, but one of these theories does offer a complementary explanation for Court actions on racial and minority cases: the input of the executive office through the solicitor general had a clear impact on the Court, as seen by the statistically significant coefficient in the first column of Table 5.1. When the solicitor general presents liberal amicus curiae briefs to the Court, this substantially increases the probability that the Supreme Court will review a case addressing racial and ethnic minority concerns. Similar to other studies (Green 1994; Kluger 1976; Tushnet 1987; Klarman 2004), I find that the actions of the solicitor general can be paramount in influencing whether a minority case is granted *certiorari*.

The other alternative factors had little influence on the Court. The number of liberal judges sitting on the bench, seen by the Court's political ideology, held little sway over its decisions. In addition, the influence minority groups wielded through submitting amicus briefs was insignificant. This finding complements other empirical studies that demonstrate a very weak link between the activities of minority groups and Supreme Court outcomes (Tauber 1998; Tauber 1999).

While minority protest was able to capitalize on public opinion to impact the cases the Court decided to review, this interactive story of influence does not carry over into the aggregate rulings rendered on these cases. As opposed to political protest behavior, the Court's ideology and the civil rights movement largely dictated justices' rulings on minority cases. These two factors are likely related, since the most liberal Court from 1960 to 1995 was that of Chief Justice Earl Warren during the civil rights era. Cases related to race were 73 percent more likely to receive a favorable ruling during the civil rights movement than in years outside of this movement period.

The results presented in Table 5.1 offer a complicated narrative of the way in which informative minority protest behavior has interacted with national perceptions of race to garner a response from the Supreme Court. The results suggest that the continuum of information provided by minority protest alone cannot shape the outcome of minority cases that are taken up by the Court. The social context of minority protest must combine with the public's perceptions on the importance of racial issues in order to help determine the types of cases the Court decides to hear. As Table 5.1 suggests, the Supreme Court was attuned to the social conditions of minority protest and how these various levels of information coalesced with public opinion.

Examining Decisions of Individual Justices

We can expound on the results discovered in the aggregate analysis. While the interaction of protest activity and public opinion was not associated with changes in the Court's aggregate decisions on race-related cases, it is possible that the individual decisions of each justice were influenced by this political phenomenon. The information-rich U.S. Supreme Court Database (Spaeth 1999) allows for an understanding of judicial responsiveness that moves the analysis from aggregate decisions to individual choices. In this section, I investigate individual justices' responses to political protest in environments when the nation saw issues of race as an important topic. The examination of individual decisions draws upon yearly data. However, some Supreme Court justices sat on the bench for only a very short period of time during the years examined (e.g., Justice Fortas for four years

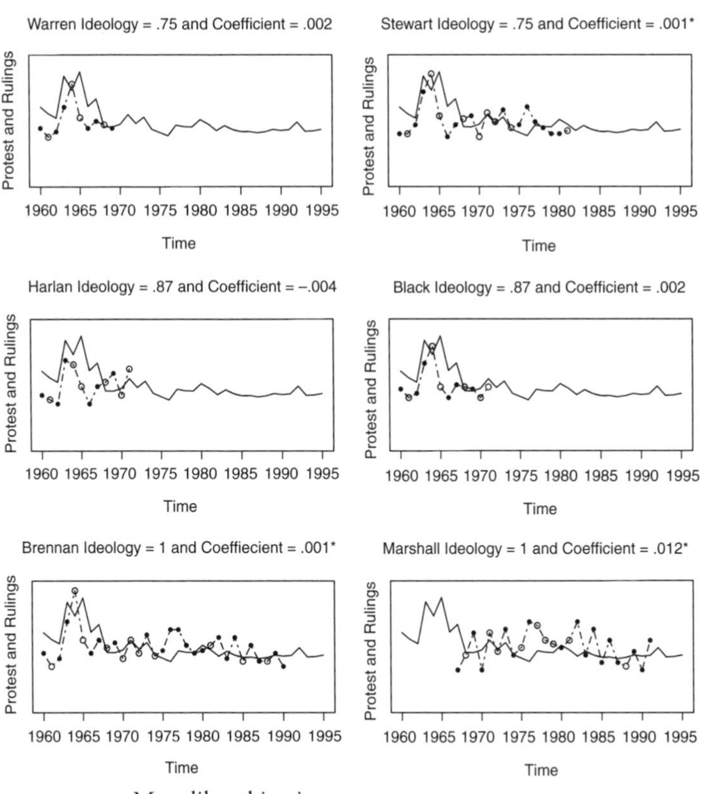

FIGURE 5.4. Most liberal justices.

and Justice Goldberg for three). Consequently, the following individual analysis considers only justices who served on the bench for a minimum of ten years in the period 1960–1995. This allows for an analysis of twelve justices, with Justice William J. Brennan Jr. serving for the longest period of time, thirty-two years. Restricting the analysis to these justices shrinks the dataset considerably; hence, the results should be viewed as suggestive rather than definitively establishing a causal link (see Mishler and Shehan 1996 for an example of a similar analysis).

To examine individual choices, several graphs are plotted showing the degree of political protest behavior that was conducted on pro-minority issues (solid line) and the percentage of minority cases on which a particular justice ruled favorably (dashed line) in Figures 5.4–5.6. The shaded dots on the dashed line indicate a year in which race relations encompassed more than 2 percent of the public agenda. The solid line for political protest behavior will remain constant for each justice, but the corresponding dashed line should fluctuate. For ease of comparison, all series are standardized. In addition, the ADL model (with a lagged dependent variable) described below was used for each justice:

$$JudicialDecisions = Protest + PublicOpinion + Protest * PublicOpinion$$

Thus, at the top of each graph the coefficient from the interaction term and its statistical significance are reported. The ideology scores are also included for comparison. The ideology score ranges from 0 to 1, where 0 represents a very conservative justice and 1 represents a very liberal justice (Segal and Cover 1989).

Figure 5.4, which considers the influence of political protest on the decisions of the most liberal justices, suggests that the information in political behavior and public opinion influenced these justices. Both Justice Marshall, a major advocate of civil rights, and Justice Brennan, one of the most liberal justices to serve on the Court, were clearly influenced by citizens' demands related to minority grievances. While this result matches well with expectations, it does raise one question. If the most liberal justices constantly supported liberal issues, should we not expect them to have supported these issues regardless of whether minority protests took place? This finding shows that while an extremely liberal justice like Marshall was likely to view minority concerns favorably, he was further emboldened in his beliefs by societal conditions that favored racial and ethnic minority concerns.

Examining the other extreme in Figure 5.5, all of the conservative justices have a negative coefficient for the interaction term. However, the majority of these results are insignificant.

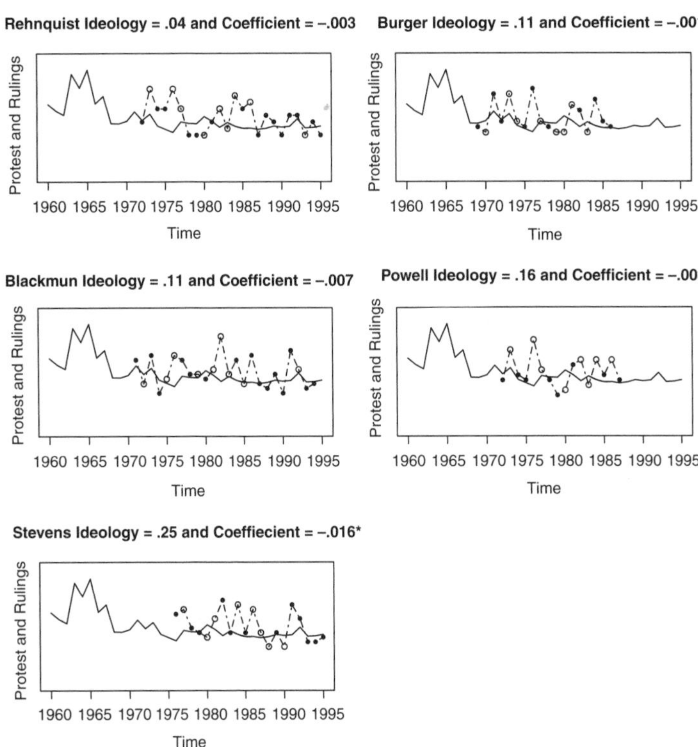

FIGURE 5.5. Most conservative justices.

The one exception is Justice John Paul Stevens, whose rulings resulted in unfavorable decisions when informative minority political protest combined with public opinion. For the most part, conservative justices appear to have made their decisions irrespective of citizens' demands regarding minority grievances, as measured by the interaction between political protest behavior and public opinion on race.

When we turn to moderate justices in Figure 5.6, we see that the story is not as lucid as those drawn from the responses of liberal and conservative justices. External information from minority protest and public opinion did not influence any of the four moderate justices. This result is surprising, given that moderate justices are less ideologically driven and might be more inclined to observe societal conditions that would

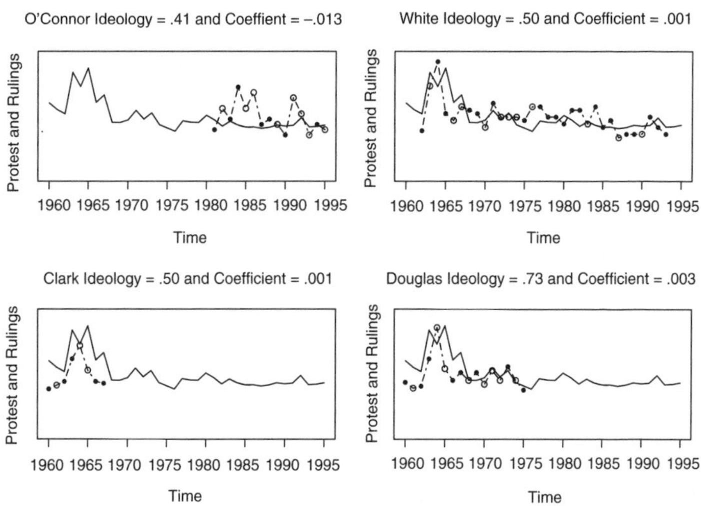

FIGURE 5.6. Most moderate justices.

inform their decisions. This would especially be expected for Justice Clark and Justice White, both of whom displayed a middle-of-the-road ideology of 0.50. Even in these cases, the signals given by informative minority protest did not tip the balance.

Conclusion

The overarching plea heard in racial and ethnic minority protest behavior has been one for equality. As organizations lend credibility, the duration of protest events expresses commitment, and contentious characteristics showcase passion, these pleas become amplified along a continuum of information and signal the importance of minority concerns. The echoing sound of public opinion is a societal demand for government to address these foremost concerns. Protesters' appeal for equality has deep roots in the judicial system and touches on one of the core duties of the Supreme Court: to administer justice by doing "equal right to the poor and to the rich." This line, drawn from the oath that every justice takes before coming to the bench, implies that justices have an obligation to behave in an equitable manner. Political protest behavior, as seen in minority protest actions, calls attention to the disproportionate number of rights violations experienced by the minority community and thus impresses upon the Supreme Court the need to recognize the effects of societal conditions on inequality. And while the Supreme Court consists of individuals who are appointed for life and insulated from the threat of reelection, the institution is part of a democratic system bound to hear and value societal concerns.

Several implications arise from this chapter. First, previous studies of political protest have suggested that citizens' political behavior can galvanize public opinion and indirectly impact political institutions (Giugni 2004; Agnone 2007; Burstein 1998; McAdam and Su 2001; Santoro 2002). In part, this chapter complements these works as they relate to the Supreme Court. However, it also refines this understanding. Minority protest can indirectly influence the cases the Court decides to review when it works in tandem with public opinion. This mediated path reflects only a marginal impact on the Supreme Court.

Second, this chapter lends credence to the notion presented by Justice Rehnquist that justices are not immune to societal changes. When we focus on individual justices, we see that the impact of changing societal conditions positively influenced some of the most liberal justices (Justices Brennan and Marshall), as well as those with a conservative ideology (Justice Clark). The response did not always lead to favorable outcomes, as illustrated by the response of Justice Stevens. The different responses from liberal and conservative justices raise the question of how personal ideology interacts with national public opinion and citizens' political actions relating to issues of race.

Finally, this chapter sharply departs from theories arguing that the role of the Supreme Court is to assure the subordination of racial minority interests by appealing to the population majority (Spann 1993). This work does not refute the majoritarian perspective that Supreme Court justices promote popular preferences. However, they do not always do so at the expense of minority interests. This is key. Working through political protest and in step with popular preferences, minority interests can affect the decisions of the Court. Consequently, this chapter offers clarity to the uncertainty voiced by Justice Marshall, quoted at the beginning of this chapter. Those who foment political protest behavior in order to bring about change on racial or ethnic minority issues must do more than simply appeal to political institutions. They must also enlist the American public.

Conclusion

Settling Protest Dust in a Post-Racial Society

You may write me down in history
With your bitter, twisted lies,
You may trod me in the very dirt
But still, like dust, I'll rise
– *Maya Angelou, "Still I Rise"*

If we accept and acquiesce in the face of discrimination, we accept the responsibility ourselves and allow those responsible to salve their conscience by believing that they have our acceptance and concurrence. We should, therefore, protest openly everything … that smacks of discrimination or slander.

– *Mary McLeod Bethune*

Political protest is a form of engagement that offers citizens an opportunity to voice their concerns. Minorities have turned to this form of political action during hard times to express their grievances to government. Piven and Cloward (1977) inform us that the benefits that follow from political protests are best realized by the economically disadvantaged and politically powerless. These are often racial and ethnic minorities (Lipsky 1970). One might conclude that racial and ethnic minorities benefit most from protest activities; this book has sought to see if, historically, they have benefited at all. Thus, this study has been guided by one central question: does minority political protest influence the actions and rhetoric of federal government?

Scholars have only recently begun to empirically investigate this link. I offered the broad critique that the literature has studied separate chains of this link in two different spheres. In one sphere, a rich examination of political actions has emerged. These studies focus on *who* engages in political action and their *motivations* for engagement. In the other sphere, countless studies of political institutions address political elites' behavior within the different branches of government. What has received less focus is the connection between minority political behavior and the national governmental response. As Chapter 1 explains, this has been due largely to the norms within the disciplines of political science and sociology to follow traditional lines of research. For the few trailblazers who have attempted to establish a direct empirical linkage between minority protest activities and federal government, the results have been rather inconclusive at best and unfounded at worst.

In contrast to traditional approaches, as well as to the conclusions of earlier research, this book has broken new ground and demonstrates a strong and direct relationship between minority appeals expressed through political protest and federal governmental action. My theory of the information continuum posits that various components of minority protest – organizational structure, contention, size, and persistence, among others – add meaning to citizens' actions. These various attributes of political protest combine to indicate the importance of minority concerns. Countermovements convey similar information, competing against pro-minority protest for issue ownership. As the salient social characteristics of one side of the issue begin to diminish in comparison to those of the other, the weaker side yields issue space and becomes overshadowed by the more significant grievances of its counterpart. Therefore, from an information continuum perspective, political protest emerges not as a uniform type of behavior but rather a series of informative signals that give politicians the cues they need to initiate policies, gauge the importance of race-related issues, and dictate the direction of their policy response.

Conceptualizing minority political protest along an information continuum provides valuable insights into the influence of citizens' behavior. It allows us to do more than determine whether a minority protest action occurred. It addresses what took place within minority behavior. This understanding of protest draws upon the social context of political protest and uses the context of citizens' actions to differentiate between the types of information being related to government and the signal strength of that information. In the latter half of the twentieth century, the information contained in political protest had a measureable effect on every branch of the national government. Whether examining the presidency, the Supreme Court, or Congress, it is evident that political protest has played a role in the formation of public policy affecting racial and ethnic minority concerns. It is important to remember, however, that its impact has affected each institution uniquely.

Congressional leaders are attuned to the information conveyed by minority political protest actions. Yet their response is apparent not in the collective actions of the legislature as it holds hearings or passes laws but rather in the roll-call votes of individual politicians. This finding brings to light a truism that has a strong foundation in the congressional literature. That is, in order to understand the behavior of legislators, scholars must examine citizen protest actions that occur within a congressional leader's district. When this is done, it becomes clear that representatives have taken a more liberal stance on racial and ethnic minority concerns when the signals they received from protest within their districts grew stronger.

The president is also responsive to citizens' preferences related to racial and ethnic minority issues, though this response varies drastically between different modes of presidential action. Presidents have often used the information in political protest to shape their public modes of executive behavior: general public statements, comments to the press, and executive orders all began to favor minority concerns as protest became more informative. To affect more grandiose modes of public presidential responsiveness, such as State of the Union addresses, however, citizens' political actions required the additional reinforcement of public opinion. In combination, informative minority protest and a rise in public concern about racial and ethnic minority issues have impressed on the president to use the most formal platform to demonstrate his resolve in addressing minority grievances.

An examination of the Supreme Court reveals a similar narrative present in the other two institutions. Minority political protest has been able to influence the type of cases that are brought to the Court. Similar to how minority protest influences presidents' State of the Union addresses, this impact is conditioned on protest's ability to occur in environments where mass public opinion views racial issues as important topics that must be addressed. And similar to the results for Congress, moreover, the impact of political protest is apparent in the individual decisions of justices but not on the Court as a collective body.

At the same time that these results suggest the complex nature of the interaction between political behavior and government, they demonstrate that political actions can bring policy gains for minorities. Protest actions were in fact vehicles of social change. They altered decisions on federal policies. When they did not change policies, they initiated the first stages of the policy-making process. And when they failed to do either of these two things, they brought protesters' concerns to bear on the minds of the public.

Reshaping Future Studies of Protest Behavior

One of the more significant implications that can be drawn from this work is that political protest has an overarching influence on the political process. The scope of this influence covers multiple activities of the federal government that include private and public responses, rhetoric and actions, and symbolic and substantive policies. Also, minority protest works differently upon the various federal institutions. The norms and procedures of each institution mediate the potential influence that protest may have on policies. Thus, in order to recognize the encompassing impact of political activism, future studies must juxtapose the influence of one branch of government against another; they will thereby offer a more complete narrative of the influence of political activism on government.

The unique empirical approach of this study has demonstrated that the link between citizens' protest activity and government is indeed quantifiable. Future research into minorities' political protest behavior that incorporates a quantitative approach is beyond valuable; it is necessary. A greater emphasis on discerning a measurable influence through a quantitative approach does not mean the reduction or demise of qualitative research on this topic. On the contrary, the quantitative and qualitative approaches must be fused together to establish a more encompassing understanding of political protest. Guarded with this dual research tactic, scholars will have fertile ground on which to study the future outcomes of protest activity.

In the end, racial and ethnic minority political protest has proven an incredible tool for citizens to elicit a response from national government officials. This begs the question: is there something special or distinct about the public's perceptions of racial issues, and of political protest attuned to these issues, that allows citizens' demands to influence government more readily than would be the case for other important topics? The answer is both yes and no. On the one hand, issues of race are similar to other issues, insofar as minorities are simply engaging in non-electoral political behavior to make their views known on an important topic. For this reason, it is likely that protest activity that addresses other issues, such as women's rights, abortion, or same-sex marriage, could have a similar effect on government when it is informative to politicians.

On the other hand, while most issues might come and go from the public agenda, the issue of race has remained one of the more resilient ones, exercising a consistent influence on government institutions since the mid-twentieth century. Racial issues have transformed political parties (Carmines and Stimson 1989), changed the rhetoric and actions of presidents (Riley 1999), and influenced the behavior of the federal courts (Flemming and Wood 1997). Race is a sensitive issue for Americans that has been molded by government and embraced through societal norms. Carmines and Stimson write: "Race, with its deep symbolic meaning in American political history, has touched a raw nerve in the body politic ... it reemerged as a partisan conflict in the early 1960's and has remained prominent since then. Thus, if a significant issue evolution is occurring in American politics, it is most likely to revolve around the issue of race" (14). Consequently, signals sent by political protest that address racial or ethnic minority concerns are not only more frequent than those for other issues, but these signals are also easily discerned by a society that has become more race-conscious over the course of American history. Thus, there *is* something unique about the issue of race.

A society that has become more sensitive to racial issues arguably produces an environment that can increase the influence of an information continuum of protest for marginal groups. [1] The historic decline of racial and ethnic minorities employing the tools of political protest is therefore perplexing. Do minorities view political protest in a different light? Have more conventional modes of political behavior, like voting, become more appealing? This line of questioning leads us to consider how citizens conceptualize the political tools they have at their disposal and how their use of these political actions has shifted over time.

[1] The legislative and moral successes of protest activities in the 1960s have made it easier for current generations to push for change (Klinkner and Smith, 1999).

From Protest to Politics ... and the Information Lost in the Process

Since the early 1970s, minority groups in the United States have shifted away from political protest and moved toward more conventional forms of political participation. The Asian American movement, which was sparked by the 1968 San Francisco Strike, witnessed Asian Americans heavily employing protest activities to express their concerns over issues ranging from the incorporation of ethnic studies courses in colleges and universities to improvements in local communities and neighborhoods (Omatsu 1994). However, Asian Americans subsequently began to shift their activities toward more conventional forms of political engagement as a way of acquiring the political power that had eluded them. Wei (1993) states, "In the 1980s, the only viable option open to Asian American activists was electoral politics. By engaging in electoral politics they ended their political isolation and purely community role" (270). The shift from unconventional political participation to more conventional forms of political engagement was further aided by the economic gains that Asian American experienced in the 1980s (Ong et al. 1994). Contemporary studies (Lien et al. 2004; Brackman and Erie 2003; Cho 1999) of Asian American politics note that this minority group is heavily engaged in conventional political activity. Yet historical accounts suggest that Asian Americans are not engaging in political protest activity as they did in the late 1960s and early 1970s.

Similarly, Latinos' heightened levels of protest activity did not continue past the 1960s. Hero (1992) argues that the movement experienced a decline in the early 1970s as political leaders strayed from protest behavior. These new leaders "stressed moderate political activities, such as voter registration, voter turnout, legal challenges to electoral obstacles, and the support of particular policies through lobbying" (Hero 1992, 39). Some authors argue that even some of the older, more aggressive organizations, such as the League of United Latin American

Citizens (LULAC), grew more conservative in the 1990s than they had been in previous years (Munoz 1989).

Protest activity has also declined among African Americans. Even in the midst of the civil rights movement, scholars suggested that blacks would shift away from protest behavior. Bayard Rustin (1965), in particular, predicted that blacks would eventually stop engaging in protest activity and move toward more conventional forms of politics. His prediction became a realization. Adolph Reed (1986) claims that black office holders have replaced black protest leaders. [2] Katherine Tate (1994) argues that not only have blacks moved away from the protest activities of the civil rights movement, but it would be difficult for them to return to such behavior because of the unfavorable political climate and the erosion of protest leadership.

The trajectory of engaging in protest behavior is similar among the three subminority groups. For each group, the 1960s and 1970s was a period during which political activism reached its zenith, followed by a decline of political protest activity in the 1980s and 1990s. While this trend is apparent for the collective minority, it has also trickled down to affect individual decisions and attitudes toward the use of protest actions. Among racial and ethnic minorities, the percentage of individuals who claimed they would never engage in a boycott, demonstration, or strike grew by more than 10 percent from 1973 to 2000 (Barnes and Kasse 1979; World Values Survey 2009). The "American protest generation" of the 1960s and 1970s has given way to a more passive generation (Jennings 1987). [3]

The decline in political protest among minorities is surprising, given the surge in Americans' use of such behavior.

[2] Manning Marable (2004) also makes the point that black leadership has moved from protest behavior to electoral politics.

[3] The lackluster political engagement of racial and ethnic minorities in the latter half of the twentieth century is partly shaped by the negative social and economic conditions of minority communities (Harris, Sinclair-Chapman, and McKenzie 2005). The unfavorable conditions of minority communities have also served to suppress other forms of non-electoral political activism that include organizational membership and community involvement.

Over the last thirty years, more Americans have turned to non-electoral behavior, such as protest actions, to express their political grievances (Inglehart and Catterberg 2002). However, the political actions of racial and ethnic minorities are not propelling this trend – far from it. By the year 2000, only 18 percent of racial and ethnic minorities had engaged in a boycott, and less than 20 percent had participated in a demonstration.[4] The average level of participation for nonminorities was higher, at 27 and 21 percent, respectively (World Values Survey 2009). Political protest is no longer, to borrow a phrase from James Scott (1985), a "weapon of the weak," but rather a form of political behavior that minorities have underused and potentially undervalued. When minorities decrease their use of this important political tool, the policy preferences they voice to government are likely to follow.

Some might argue that minority protest actions have served their purpose and would be less helpful today as a method of resolving minority concerns. But the implication drawn from the information continuum theory posits the opposite point: because minorities have shifted away from political protest, politicians have actually become less informed about the importance of addressing race relations. Lackluster graduation rates of black and Latino students, startlingly high incarceration numbers in African American communities, and unemployment figures that are twice the national average have become passive and mundane topics where a problem is widely recognized but little governmental attention has been given to address these issues. This is not because these issues are unimportant topics. It is instead, at least in part, because racial and ethnic minorities have shifted away from political protest and therefore are failing to indicate to government the salience of their grievances. It is on this point that the true value of this work emerges and drastically deviates from

[4] However, Jennifer Hochschild (2006, 490) argues that black Americans will use protest actions to combat inequality when they perceive "American race relations to be sufficiently improved that racial solidarity is not the primary value to which they must always attend."

contemporary perspectives of minority protest and its influence on government.

The sole devotion to electoral politics has stagnated racial progress. To be clear, I do not look to discredit electoral actions. On the contrary, it is one of the only forms of political action that assures a stake in institutionalized politics. However, there are certain limitations presented through the electoral process that hinder minorities' communication to government. First, elections are temporally confined. In the best-case scenario, minorities vote only once a year. However, the other 364 days ought not be an extended sabbatical away from communicating with government; such an approach provides politicians with incomplete information. A citizen's vote offered during an election is a general acquiescence to a politician's complete platform, but platforms change as politicians adapt to the shifting social and political climate. Election results, potentially taken years in advance, offer little counsel to a politician addressing evolving problems that present new challenges. Elections thus offer only a snapshot of minorities' changing preferences.

Second, electoral politics in a democratic system is by nature a majoritarian construct. Political candidates require a majority of votes to be successful. Thus, even if racial and ethnic minorities vote as a coherent bloc, they still require a segment of nonminority constituents to join their ranks in order to elect their preferred candidate or policy at the voting booth. This electoral design that relies on majoritarian preferences diminishes the impact that minorities can have on government (Guinier 1994). It is no surprise that author Zoltan Hajnal (2009) finds that African Americans, more than other groups in society, have constantly walked away from Election Day as electoral losers, meaning they are less likely to elect a winning political candidate and therefore less represented in American democracy.[5]

5 Hajnal (2009) found that 41 percent of black voters were "superlosers," meaning they voted for the losing candidate in the presidential, senatorial, and gubernatorial elections. Only 9 percent of white American voters had similar misfortune.

That said, the remedy for increasing minority political representation does not lie in abandoning electoral politics. Nor is there solace in focusing solely on another mode of political behavior, a strategy that would be equally as egregious an error as only voting. Rather, minorities must pick up the ballot *and* the banner. In other words, the best path of engagement to increase racial progress would combine voting activity with protest behavior. Voting will place the most qualified politicians in the legislative and executive branches, while protest behavior will offer these politicians greater insight into the complexities of minority issues. The benefits of such political protest would also be recognized by the Supreme Court and incorporated in its rulings, even though justices' life tenure makes them unaffected by the electoral process.

The Future Political Landscape: Minority Protest in a Post-Racial Society

On January 20, 2009, Barack Obama became the first African American president of the United States. His electoral victory offered encouragement and hope to minorities. As a political figure, he extended the possibilities for minorities to influence government, and as an individual he was the quintessential role model for young minorities. What seemed inconceivable just fifty years earlier had become nightly news. Obama's presidency also had a profound paradoxical implication that questioned the role of race in the nation. The election of a racial minority challenged notions of racial hierarchy, inherent racial inferiority, and inequality. The disadvantages presented by one's skin tone seemed less of a barrier after the election. If the consideration of race was not on the precipice of becoming extinct in the eyes of many Americans, it had surely been reduced to near-irrelevance. This perception has lingered to become a growing view of many that conceive of the United States as a "post-racial society."

The idealist notion that America has arrived at a post-racial society is noble in its aspiration, but it outpaces the persisting harsh realities of life in many minority communities. The unsettling statistics presented earlier on the disproportionate rates of education, high incarceration levels, and low income status among racial and ethnic minorities are only a few indicators that race remains an indispensable component for understanding societal conditions. With such inequalities looming in American society, it is difficult for the United States to be credibly deemed "post-racial" after one election. In 2008 during a National Convention Center speech, right before he was elected president, then-Senator Obama expressed this sentiment: "I have never been so naïve as to believe that we can get beyond our racial divisions in a single election cycle, or with a single candidacy" (Obama 2009). Nevertheless, perceptions shape reality. In one year's time, from July 2008 to April 2009, the proportion of Americans who felt that race relations were "good" catapulted from 53 to 66 percent (Stolberg and Connelly 2009). Federal politicians can look at these perceptions as offering strong cues to support decreasing their efforts to address minority concerns.

In an environment in which attitudes toward the status of race as a national problem do not line up with the realities of racial inequality, protest actions become even more significant. Minority protest actions can serve as an equalizer that closes the gap between perceptions of minority status and the reality of the conditions in which minorities live. The information expressed through the scope of protest signals the true gravity of minority concerns.

In the new post-racial frontier, politicians have not lacked information stemming from protest behavior. Obama's ascendance to power also produced the Tea Party movement, which can be understood as a conservative populist movement expressing discontent with federal policies. This movement has made significant inroads into the political party system. If the changing rhetoric of federal politicians is not evidence enough, then the landslide victory of the Republican Party in the 2010 midterm elections should stand as a strong confirmation that the Tea Party, through its protest actions, became a powerful force in the political arena. Undoubtedly, the information continuum that I laid out in this book switched in the negative direction with the rise of this movement. That is to say, politicians as well as the mass public were being informed by protest behavior, but the signals stemming from these political activities encapsulated a conservative message, one that was unlikely to accord with the liberal concerns of racial and ethnic minorities.

Conclusion

The title of this chapter, "Settling Protest Dust and Governmental Success," references the state of affairs after hundreds of thousands of protesters have descended upon Washington, DC, state capitols, and even local establishments that infringed upon minority rights. In the aftermath of decades of minority appeals to government, the euphemistic phrase "settling protest dust" simply poses the question of whether political behavior has made a difference in the lives of racial and ethnic minorities. This book suggests that, overall, it has. In this respect, its conclusions are in line with numerous historical perspectives, anecdotal accounts in scholarly work, and even informal conclusions reached at water-cooler discussions. But what sets this book apart is its deeper understanding of *why* federal politicians would be influenced by citizen activism. In order to understand the value of protest behavior, one must consider the social characteristics of the protest actions that gave meaning to citizens' behavior. Minority protest actions backed by prominent organizational support that drew large numbers of protesters, persisted over time, and involved contentious behavior captured attention for their causes. They alerted the federal government of new issues that were gaining ground. And because the social characteristics of minority protest overshadowed voices from the other side, pro-minority concerns dominated the issue space and offered signals to the federal government on how best to direct its response.

For these reasons, protest activity is integral to the fabric of American democracy. Martin Luther King Jr., in referring to lunch counter sit-ins, put this best in a speech he offered on the eve of his assassination: "I knew that as they were sitting in, they were really standing up for the best in the American Dream. And taking the whole nation back to those great wells of democracy which were dug deep by the Founding Fathers in the Declaration of Independence and the Constitution." While not ingrained into the formal institutional channels of influence, political protest is essential to American democracy. As politicians seek out the information that is vital for governance, protest behavior communicates the concerns of the public. Thus, this book concludes on an optimistic note. Protests are not relics of the past that should lie fallow in our political toolbox, but rather are instruments of democratic change.

Appendix A

Defining Minority Political Protest

The heart of this volume's assessment of minority protest comes from the Dynamics of Collective Action database. The DCA includes what is arguably the most extensive existing coverage of collective behavior. It includes data on incidents of protest collected from daily reports of the *New York Times* from 1960 through 1995, encompassing over twenty-one thousand protest events coded by date, event type, target of protest, grievances expressed, and other contextual information on the protest action (size, organizations involved, contentious actions, and more).[1] This NSF-funded project led by Doug McAdam, John McCarthy, Susan Olzak, and Sarah Soule has been widely used to understand protest behavior.[2] The abundance of information it offers allows me to examine protest actions over a contentious period of time for race relations. It also helps me to explain how government's response

[1] Because of the *New York Times'* national syndication and willingness to cover minority protest events in the 1960s when other newspaper sources refused to report on this behavior, it is a good source of information to assess protest activity in the second half of the twentieth century. Chapter 2 presents a more detailed discussion of the benefits and limitations of using the *Times*.

[2] Just a few of the notable projects that use this data include McAdam and Su 2002; Earl, Soule, and McCarthy 2003; King and Soule 2007; Olzak and Soule 2009; and Soule and Davenport 2009.

to various forms of political protest has changed in the post–civil rights era.

Using the Dynamics of Collective Action dataset, I assemble protest behavior from the following activities: demonstrations, rallies, marches, vigils, picketing, civil disobedience, information distributions, riots, strikes, and boycotts. Second, I focused only on protest events that targeted government. Finally, I declared protest events as *minority* protest actions based upon the issues that were voiced as opposed to the racial and ethnic identity of the group. The following general issues were used to capture racial and ethnic minority concerns: discrimination, civil rights, voting rights, minority unemployment, welfare, immigration, and education of the underprivileged.

Table A.1 separates the various characteristics that were used to create the continuum score. A slight majority of racial and ethnic minority protests included an arrest (53 percent). Other contentious attributes of protest, such as the presence of police and reports of violence (representing 36 percent and 17 percent of protests, respectively), encompassed a large number of minority activities. These figures might lead some to view protests as only being a violent contentious action. This is a misconception. Indeed, the second largest component of protest actions was the support of interest group. An interest group was involved in 43 percent of all protest actions over this time period. This less contentious component of political protest served to mobilize minority groups and provide valuable resources, which was critical to implementing change. Other moderate actions such as a protest lasting more than a day or more than 100 individuals being present at a protest event (10 percent and 15 percent, respectively) occurred more often than injuries, property damage, and deaths.

Table A.2 illustrates the total number of three types of protest over the course of a year: (1) the total number of

TABLE A.1. *Characteristics of minority protest, 1960–1995*

Characteristics of Minority Protest	Percent of Protests
Death occurs	0.02
Reports of property damage	0.10
Reports of injury	0.10
Lasts longer than a day	0.11
Larger than 100 people	0.15
Reports of violence	0.17
Police are initially present	0.36
Support of political organization	0.43
An arrest was made	0.53

minority protests, the information continuum score for all minority protests, and the total number of protests regardless of issue (i.e., minority and nonminority protests). The information continuum score displays a similar trend to the total number of minority protests, and there is 97 percent correlation between both columns. However, the continuum scores capture certain components of protest that are not seen by the total number of minority protests reported in column one. Consider the year 1967, for example. While the total number of minority protest declines from 1966 to 1967, the continuum score actually increases and is likely responding to the contentious riots that occurred over this time period. Or consider protests events that occurred in 1976. While there were a total of forty minority protests in this year, roughly half of these protests were conducted by counterdemonstrators that did not support racial and ethnic minority concerns. The competing voices lowered the continuum score to one. Table A.2 helps to understand how a continuum score of minority protest relate to simple counts of minority activism as well as to the general trend of overall protest behavior.

TABLE A.2. *Minority protests, continuum scores, and overall protests, 1960–1995*

Year	Minority Protests	Minority Protest Continuum Scores	Total Protests
1960	199	277	834
1961	168	213	606
1962	147	171	468
1963	375	574	909
1964	249	437	755
1965	368	615	1033
1966	189	283	936
1967	164	356	838
1968	60	88	772
1969	46	86	998
1970	76	111	813
1971	121	205	812
1972	70	120	707
1973	91	181	680
1974	44	65	415
1975	56	33	501
1976	40	1	478
1977	65	103	738
1978	70	89	634
1979	60	86	944
1980	89	157	773
1981	71	112	687
1982	36	51	498
1983	64	99	551
1984	43	62	542
1985	44	42	673
1986	30	43	526
1987	34	30	493
1988	33	40	465
1989	35	62	510
1990	50	52	572
1991	46	59	578
1992	77	133	488
1993	48	44	483
1994	36	48	404
1995	44	62	501

Appendix B

Study Description and Coding Across Multiple Institutions

I use a variety of sources to understand a collective response from national government. A description of the variables used for each institution is described below. Measures of public opinion and the civil rights movement are constantly included in the analysis of each institution. Thus, I begin with these universal variables.

Public Opinion: Using the Gallup's Most Important Problem series, I code the percentage of respondents who felt that racial and ethnic minority concerns were the most important problems facing the nation. This is used as a thermometer to gauge the relevance of racial issues.

Civil Rights Movement: The civil rights movement is dated from 1960 to 1968. Naturally, there are events that took place in the 1950s, a time period I believe to be a part of the civil rights movement, that are not included in this study. The use of 1960 is simply a byproduct of the available data on political protest. The year 1968 is selected as the end of this period because it coincides with the death of Dr. Martin Luther King Jr., which fragmented the movement. Moreover, this year is often considered to have signaled the decline of movement activism (see Lawson and Payne 1998).

Congress

Congressional Hearings: Drawn from the *Policy Agendas Project*, this is a measure of the total number of hearings held by Congress that addressed the following issues: ethnic minority and racial group discrimination, civil rights issues, voting rights, food stamps and food assistance programs, poverty and assistance for low-income families, immigration and refugee issues, and education of underprivileged students.

Public Laws: Drawn from the *Policy Agendas Project*, this is a measure of the total number of public laws passed in each year that address the following issues: ethnic minority and racial group discrimination, civil rights issues, voting rights, food stamps and food assistance programs, poverty and assistance for low-income families, immigration and refugee issues, and education of underprivileged students.

Divided Government: This measures when the president's party did not control both chambers of Congress. When this occurred, this variable is coded as 1. For other periods, it is coded 0.

Minorities in Congress: This is an overall count of the number of members in each congressional session who considered themselves to be of a racial and/or ethnic background. Names were taken from the listing of minority congressional members produced by the *Congressional Research Service* (Manning and Shogan 2010; Tong 2011).

Roll-Call Votes: I used the roll-call votes classified as minority issues by Keith Poole and Howard Rosenthal (1997), as well as those from David Rohde (2010). In combining both classifications, I examine a comprehensive list of congressional bills involving the following general issues: discrimination, civil rights, desegregation, bussing, affirmative action, immigration, food stamps/food programs, minority unemployment, and low-income housing (see Chapter 3 for a lengthier discussion of the creation of minority roll-call votes).

Black Representative: I code representatives as 1 if they considered themselves a Black American. Other members of Congress are coded as 0.

Latino Representative: I code representatives as 1 if they consider themselves a Hispanic American. Other members of Congress are coded as 0.

Democratic Party: This variable is coded as 1 if the representative belongs to the Democratic Party and 0 otherwise.

Length of Service: This is a measure of the number of years a congressional leader has served in the House of Representatives.

Percent of Democrats: This measures the percent of the Democratic vote share that a representative received in the previous election.

Southern Districts: I code the districts in the South with 1, and all other districts receive a 0. I use districts that fall within the following southern states: Alabama, Georgia, Florida, Louisiana, Mississippi, North Carolina, South Carolina, and Tennessee.

Incumbent: This measures whether a district has reelected a sitting congressional representative, which I code as 1, or if this is a representative's first time being elected to the House of Representatives, which I code as 0.

Minority Population in a District: This measures the total number of black and Latino citizens who reside in a congressional district, as reported by the U.S. Census.

Black Population in a District: This measures the total number of black citizens who reside in a congressional district, as reported by the U.S. Census.

President

In order to examine the president's attention to racial and ethnic concerns, I searched an electronic collection of the volumes of the *Public Papers of the Presidents* series published by the Office of the Federal Register, which is a part of the *American Presidency Data Project* (Woolley and Peters 2008), for documents relating to minority issues. Table B.1 provides the presidential action alongside the list of keywords that were used to narrow down the list of documents containing words potentially related to racial issues. With the aid of two research assistants, each entry returned from the keyword search was later read for its content to assure that the information was relevant to minority concerns. Documents wherein the president addressed a racial or ethnic concern, taking a favorable or neutral position, were coded as a 1; otherwise, the document was coded with a 0. Given that the State of the Union address is only offered once a year, each sentence of the annual address that related to racial issues was coded with a 1, and non-race-related sentences were coded with a 0.

Democratic President: This measure is coded as 1 when the president belonged to the Democratic Party and 0 when he belonged to the Republican Party.

Democratic Congress: This measures periods of time when Democratic congressional leaders consisted of the majority in both the House and the Senate.

Divided Government: I code this variable based upon when the president's party did not control both chambers of Congress. Periods when the presidents' party did not control both chambers are coded as 1. All other periods are coded 0.

Presidential Approval: As reported by the Gallup Poll, this is the percentage of individuals who approve of the job the president is doing. When I examine quarterly data, this measure is the average approval rating across all the polls collected over a three-month period. Similarly, when I examine yearly data, this measure is the average approval rating across all the polls taken in a year.

TABLE B.1. *Keywords to search presidential public papers*

Presidential Action	Keywords
Presidential letter	Letters, note, civil rights, protest, discrimination, integration, minority, black, negro, African American, Hispanic, Latino, Chicano, Asian, movement, demonstration, march, boycott, riot, immigration, underprivileged, welfare, low-income, racial, diversity
Memorandum	Memorandum, memo, orders, civil rights, protest, discrimination, integration, minority, black, negro, African American, Hispanic, Latino, Chicano, Asian, movement, demonstration, march, boycott, riot immigration, underprivileged, welfare, low-income, racial, diversity
Statements	Signing statements, statements, comments, response, civil rights, protest, discrimination, integration, minority, black, negro, African American, Hispanic, Latino, Chicano, Asian, movement, demonstration, march, riot, boycott, immigration, underprivileged, welfare, low-income, racial, diverse
Press conferences	Press, news, media, conferences, television, report, civil rights, protest, discrimination, integration, minority, black, negro, African American, Hispanic, Latino, Chicano, Asian, movement, demonstration, march, boycott, riot, immigration, underprivileged, welfare, low-income, diversity
Executive order	Executive, orders, mandate, law, legislation, civil rights, protest, discrimination, integration, minority, black, negro, African American, Hispanic, Latino, Chicano, Asian, movement, demonstration, march, boycott, riot, immigration, underprivileged, welfare, low-income, diversity
State of the Union	(All State of the Union address from 1955–1992 were read.)

Supreme Court

Minority Cases: This measures the percentage of cases the Supreme Court decided to review that addressed the following topics: the Voting Rights Act of 1965 (plus amendments), desegregation, affirmative action, reapportionment, poverty law (welfare benefits), immigration and naturalization, deportation, and sit-in demonstrations.

Minority Rulings: This measures the percentage of minority cases on which the Supreme Court offered a liberal ruling.

Court Ideology: This measures the mean ideological score of the Court, derived from the average of Segal and Cover's (1989) measures for each justice's ideology. Higher values indicate the Court is more liberal, and lower values indicate it is more conservative.[1]

Amicus Curiae: This measures the annual number of liberal amicus briefs submitted to the Supreme Court by special interest groups and political associations.

Solicitor General: This measures the annual number of liberal amicus brief the solicitor general submitted to the Supreme Court.

Public Mood: This measures the three-to-five-year moving average detailing the liberal or conservative views of the nation. Higher values indicate the mood of the nation is leaning liberal, whereas lower or negative values indicate it is more conservative.

[1] Care was taken in aggregating ideological scores for a complete calendar year. The reason for this is that the Court only convenes from the first of October until mid to late June. Thus, a change in justices could result in a different ideological court from January to June than from October to December. When this situation occurs, I take the average of the two ideological Courts.

Appendix C

Time Series Methods

A two-stage autoregressive distributed lagged (ADL) model is the main regression technique used in this study to capture the numerical influence that protest has on governmental actions. It is referred to as a "two-stage" process because the ADL is first used to understand the influence that an information continuum of protest has on mass public opinion regarding the importance of race (see Chapter 2). The first-stage equation is as follows:

$$Z_t^{Opinion} = \alpha_0 + \alpha_1 Z_{t-1} + \alpha_2 X_t^{Protest} + \alpha_3 X_{t-1} + \varepsilon_t$$

In the second stage, the ADL model is then used to assess the response from government. However, the predicted probabilities of public opinion taken from the first ADL model are incorporated in the second stage as mass preferences that have been indirectly influenced by protest (see Chapters 3–5).

$$\begin{aligned} Y_t^{Government\ Action} &= \beta_0 + \beta_1 Y_{t-1} + \beta_2 X_t^{Protest} \\ &+ \beta_3 X_{t-1} + \beta_4 \hat{Z}_t^{Opinion} + \beta_5 Z_{t-1} + \varepsilon_t \end{aligned}$$

The two-stage approach allows us to observe the direct impact of protest, as well as the mediated influence of protest that is working through public opinion.

I used a nonrestrictive general ADL model at each stage of the analysis to assess how much protest's influence is distributed over time. This meant that lags of protest and governmental responsive were always included to consider the immediate and delayed impact of a protest continuum. As Chapters 3 through 5 illustrate, the response from government was rarely delayed, occurring in the same three-month period or the same congressional and Supreme Court sessions as protest actions.

References

1954. *Brown v. Board of Education*. 347 U.S. 483.
1960. *Boynton v. Virginia*. 364 U.S. 454.
1963. *Edwards v. South Carolina*. 373 U.S. 229.
1965a. *Louisiana v. United States*. 380 U.S. 145.
1965b. *Watson v. City of Memphis*. 373 U.S. 526.
1967. *Loving v. Virginia*. 388 U.S. 1.
1978. *Regents of the University of California V. Bakke*. 438 U.S. 265.

Achen, Christopher. 1975. "Mass Political Attitudes and the Survey Response." *American Political Science Review* 69:1218–31.

Agnone, Jon. 2007. "Amplifying Public Opinion: The Policy Impact of the U.S. Environmental Movement." *Social Forces* 85:1593–620.

Albritton, Robert B. 1979. "A Reply to Piven and Cloward." *American Political Science Review* 73:1020–23.

Amenta, Edwin. 2006. *When Movements Matter: The Townsend Plan and the Rise of Social Security*. Princeton, NJ: Princeton University Press.

Amenta, Edwin, and Neal Caren. 2004. "The Legislative, Organizational, and Beneficiary Consequences of State-Oriented Challengers." In *The Blackwell Companion to Social Movements*, ed. David Snow, Sarah Soul, and Hanspeter Kriesi. London: Blackwell.

Amenta, Edwin, Neal Caren, Elizabeth Chiarello, and Yang Su. 2010. "The Political Consequences of Social Movements." *Annual Review of Sociology* 36:287–307.

Andrews, Kenneth. 2001. "Social Movements and Policy Implementation: The Mississippi Civil Rights Movement and the War on Poverty, 1965–1971." *American Sociological Review* 66:71–95.

2004. *Freedom is a Constant Struggle: The Mississippi Civil Rights Movement and Its Legacy*. Chicago: University of Chicago Press.

Arnold, R. Douglas. 1990. *The Logic of Congressional Action*. New Haven, CT: Yale University Press.

Ashmore, Harry. 1994. *Civil Rights and Wrongs: A Memoir of Race and Politics 1944–1994*. New York: Pantheon Books.

Austen-Smith, David, and John Wright. 1994. "Counteractive Lobbying." *American Journal of Political Science* 38:25–44.

Babb, Sarah. 1996. "A True American System of Finance: Frame Resonance in the U.S. Labor Movement, 1866–1896." *American Sociological Review* 61:1033–52.

Bachrach, Peter, and Morton Baratz. 1962. "Two Faces of Power." *American Political Science Review* 56:947–52.

Bailey, Michael, Brian Kamoie, and Forrest Maltzman. 2005. "Signals From the Tenth Justice: The Political Role of the Solicitor General in Supreme Court Decision Making." *American Journal of Political Science* 49:72–85.

Baird, Vanessa. 2004. "The Effect of Politically Salient Decisions on the U.S. Supreme Court's Agenda." *Journal of Politics* 66:755–72.

Baker, Andy, and Corey Cook. 2005. "Representing Black Interests and Promoting Black Culture: The Importance of African American Descriptive Representation in the U.S. House." *DuBois Review* 2:227–46.

Banks, Jeffrey. 1999. "Committee Proposals and Restrictive Rules." *Proceedings of the National Academy of Sciences* 96:8295–300.

Barnes, Samuel H., and Max Kasse. 1979. Political Action: Mass Participation in Five Western Democracies. Sage Publications.

Bartels, Larry. 1991. "Constituency Opinion and Congressional Policy Making: The Reagan Defense Buildup." *American Political Science Review* 85:457–74.

Baum, Lawrence. 1988. "Measuring Policy Change in the U.S. Supreme Court." *The American Political Science Review* 82:905–12.

2010. *The Supreme Court*. Washington, DC: CQ Press.

Baumgartner, Frank, and Bryan Jones. 1993. *Agendas and Instability in American Politics*. Chicago: University of Chicago Press.

Baumgartner, Frank, Bryan Jones, and Michael MacLeod. 2000. "The Evolution of Legislative Jurisdictions." *Journal of Politics* 62:321–49.

Baumgartner, Frank R., and Christine Mahoney. 2005. *Social Movements, the Rise of New Issues, and the Public Agenda*. Minneapolis: University of Minnesota Press.

Beck, Nathaniel, and Jonathan Katz. 1995. "What to Do (and Not to Do) With Time-Series Cross-Section Data." *American Political Science Review* 89:634–47.

2001. "Throwing Out the Baby with the Bath Water: A Comment on Green, Kim and Yoon." *International Organizations* 55:487–95.

2004. "Random Coefficient Models for Time-Series-Cross-Section Data." Social Science Working Paper 1205, Division of the

Humanities and Social Sciences, California Institute of Technology, September, 2004.

Bell, Derrick. 1979. "Bakke, Minority Admissions, and the Usual Price of Racial Remedies." *California Law Review* 67:3–19.

Bent, Devin. 1982. "Partisan Elections and Public Policy: Response to Black Demands in Large American Cities." *Journal of Black Studies* 12:291–314.

Black, Merle. 1978. "Racial Composition of Congressional Districts and Support for Federal Voting Rights in the American South." *Social Science Quarterly* 59:435–50.

Blasi, Vincent. 1983. *The Burger Court: The Counter-Revolution That Wasn't*. New Haven, CT Yale University Press.

Bonastia, Chris. 2000. "Why Did Affirmative Action in Housing Fail During the Nixon Era? Exploring the 'Institutional Home' of Social Policies." *Social Problems* 47:523–42.

Brackman, Harold, and Steven Erie. 2003. "Beyond 'Politics By Other Means'? Empowerment Strategies for Los Angeles' Asian Pacific Community." In *Asian American Politics: Law, Participation, and Policy*, ed. Don T. Nakanishi and James S. Lai. New York: Rowman and Littlefield.

Branch, Taylor. 1989. *Parting the Waters: America in the King Years, 1954–63*. New York: Simon and Schuster.

1999. *Pillar of Fire: America in the King Years, 1963–65*. New York: Simon and Schuster.

Brennan, William. 1973. "Justice Brennan Calls National Court of Appeals Proposal 'Fundamentally Unnecessary and Ill Advised'." *American Bar Association Journal* 59:835–40.

Browning, Rufus, Dale Marshall, and David Tabb. 1986. "Protest Is Not Enough: A Theory of Political Incorporation." *PS* 19:576–81.

Browning, Rufus P., Dale Rogers Marshall, and David H. Tabb. 1984. *Protest Is Not Enough*. Berkeley: University of California Press.

Bullock, Charles. 1981. "Congressional Voting and the Mobilization of a Black Electorate in the South." *Journal of Politics* 43:662–82.

Burstein, Paul. 1998. *Discrimination, Jobs, and Politics: The Struggle for Equal Employment Opportunity in the United States Since the New Deal*. Chicago: University of Chicago Press.

1999. "Social Movements and Public Policy." In *How Social Movements Matter*, ed. Marco Giugni, Doug McAdam, and Charles Tilly. Minneapolis: University of Minnesota Press.

Button, James. 1989. *Blacks and Social Change: Impact of the Civil Rights Movement in Southern Communities*. Princeton: NJ: Princeton University Press.

Caldeira, Gregory A., and James L. Gibson. 1992. "Blacks and the United States Supreme Court: Models of Diffuse Support." *The Journal of Politics* 54:1120–45.

Cameron, Charles, David Epstein, and Sharyn O'Halloran. 1996. "Do Majority-Minority Districts Maximize Substantive Black Representation in Congress." *American Political Science Review* 90:794–812.

Campbell, Andrea Louise. 2003. *How Policies Make Citizens: Senior Political Activism and the American Welfare State*. Princeton, NJ: Princeton University Press.

Canes-Wrone, Brandice, and Kenneth Shotts. 2004. "The Conditional Nature of Presidential Responsiveness to Public Opinion." *American Journal of Political Science* 48:690–706.

Canes-Wrone, Brandice, Michael Herron, and Kenneth Shotts. 2001. "Leadership and Pandering: A Theory of Executive Policymaking." *American Journal of Political Science* 44:532–50.

Canon, Bradley. 1992. "The Supreme Court as a Cheerleader in Politico-Moral Disputes." *The Journal of Politics* 54:637–53.

Canon, David T. 1999. *Race, Redistricting, and Representation: The Unintended Consequences of Black-Majority Districts*. Chicago: University of Chicago Press.

Caplan, Lincoln. 1987. *The Tenth Justice*. New York: Knopf.

Carmines, Edward, and James Stimson. 1989. *Issue Evolution: Race and the Transformation of American Politics*. Princeton, NJ: Princeton University Press.

Carter, Jimmy. 1978. "Telecommunications Minority Assistance Program Announcement of Administration Program." *The American Presidency Project*. http://www.presidency.ucsb.edu/ws/?pid=29917

1980. "Sterling, Virginia Remarks on Signing the Education Amendments of 1980 Into Law." *The American Presidency Project*. http://www.presidency.ucsb.edu/ws/?pid=45205

Cho, Wendy K Tam. 1999. "Naturalization, Socialization, Participation: Immigrants and (Non-) Voting." *Journal of Politics* 61:1140–55.

Chong, Dennis. 1991. *Collective Action and the Civil Rights Movement*. Chicago: University of Chicago Press.

Cohen, Jeffery. 1995. "Presidential Rhetoric and the Public Agenda." *American Journal of Political Science* 39:87–107.

Cohen, Jeffrey. 1997. *Presidential Responsiveness and Public Policy-Making*. Ann Arbor: University of Michigan.

Collier, Aldore. 1992. "Maxine Waters: Telling It Like It Is in L.A." *Ebony* 47:35–41.

Combs, Michael W., John Hibbing, and Susan Welch. 1984. "Black Constituents and Congressional Roll Call Votes." *Western Political Quarterly* 37:424–34.

Converse, Philip. 1964. "The Nature of Belief Systems in Mass Publics." In *Ideology and Discontent*, ed. David E. Apter. New York: Free Press.

Cooper, Phillip J. 2002. *By Order of the President: The Use and Abuse of Executive Direct Action*. Lawrence: University Press of Kansas.

Cress, Daniel, and David Snow. 2000. "The Outcomes of Homeless Mobilization: The Influence of Organization, Disruption, Political Mediation, and Framing." *American Journal of Sociology* 105:1063–104.

Davenport, Christian. 2010. *Media Bias, Perspective and State Repression: The Black Panther Party*. Cambridge: Cambridge University Press.

Davenport, Christian, Sarah Soule, and David Armstrong. 2011. "Protesting While Black? The Differential Policing of American Activism, 1960 to 1990." *American Sociological Review* 76:152–76.

Earl, Jennifer, Sarah Soule, and John McCarthy. 2003. "Protest Under Fire? Explaining the Policing of Protest." *American Sociological Review* 68:581–606.

Edwards, George, William Mitchell, and Reed Welch. 1995. "Explaining Presidential Approval: The Significance of Issue Salience." *American Journal of Political Science* 39:108–34.

Edwards, George C., and B. Dan Wood. 1999. "Who Influences Whom? The President, Congress, and the Media." *American Political Science Review* 93:327–44.

Eisinger, Peter. 1973. "The Conditions of Protest Behavior in American Cities." *The American Political Science Review* 67:11–28.

Ely, John. 1980. *Democracy and Distrust: A Theory of Judicial Review*. Cambridge, MA: Harvard University Press.

Erikson, Robert, Wright Gerald, and McIver John. 1993. *Statehouse Democracy: Public Opinion and Policy in the American States*. Cambridge, MA: Harvard University Press.

Erikson, Robert S., Michael B. Mackuen, and James A. Stimson. 2002. *The Macro Polity (Cambridge Studies in Public Opinion and Political Psychology)*. Cambridge University Press.

Escobar, Edward. 1993. "The Dialects of Repression: The Los Angeles Police Department and the Chicano Movement, 1968–1971." *The Journal of American History* 79:1483–514.

Fenno, Richard. 1978. *Home Style*. New York: HarperCollins.

Fleisher, Richard. 1993. "Explaining the Change in Roll-Call Voting of Southern Democrats." *Journal of Politics* 55:327–41.

Flemming, Roy, and B. Dan Wood. 1997. "The Public and the Supreme Court: Individual Justice Responsiveness to American Policy Moods." *American Journal of Political Science* 41:468–98.

Fording, Richard. 1997. "The Conditional Effect of Violence as a Political Tactic: Mass Insurgency, Electoral Context and Welfare Generosity in the American States." *American Journal of Political Science* 41:1–29.

Funston, Richard. 1975. "The Supreme Court and Critical Elections." *American Political Science Review* 69:795–811.

Gamson, William. 1975. *The Strategy of Social Protest*. Homewood, IL: Dorsey Press.

1992. *Talking Politics*. Cambridge: Cambridge University Press.

Garcia, Chris, and Rudolph de la Garza. 1977. *The Chicano Political Experience*. North Scituate, MA: Duxbury.

Gay, Claudine. 2007. "Legislating Without Constraints: The Effect of Minority Districting on Legislators' Responsiveness to Constituency Preferences." *Journal of Politics* 69:442–56.

Geer, John. 1996. *From Tea Leaves to Opinion Polls*. New York: Columbia University Press.

Gibson, James, and Gregory Caldeira. 1992. "Blacks and the United States Supreme Court: Models of Diffuse Support." *Journal of Politics* 54:1121–45.

Giugni, Marco. 2004. *Social Protest and Policy Change: Ecology, Antinuclear, and Peace Movements in Comparative Perspective*. Lanham, MD: Rowman and Littlefield.

2007. "Useless Protest? A Time-Series Analysis of the Policy Outcomes of Ecology, Antinuclear, and Peace Movements in the United States, 1977–1995." *Mobilization: An International Quarterly* 12:53–77.

Gosnell, Harold. 1948. *Democracy: The Threshold of Freedom*. New York: Ronald Press Company.

Graham, Barbara. 2002. "Executive-Judicial Interaction as a Factor in Explaining Presidential Policy Making." *Presidential Studies Quarterly* 32:509–30.

2003. "Explaining Supreme Court Policymaking in Civil Rights: The Influence of the Solicitor General, 1953–2002." *The Policy Studies Journal* 31:253–71.

Green, Jack. 1994. *Crusaders in the Court: How a Dedicated Band of Lawyers Fought for the Civil Rights Revolution*. New York: Basic Books.

Gronke, Paul, Jeffrey Koch, and J. Matthew Wilson. 2003. "Follow the Leader? Presidential Approval, Presidential Support, and Representatives' Electoral Fortunes." *The Journal of Politics* 65:785–808.

Guinier, Lani. 1994. *The Tyranny of the Majority: Fundamental Fairness in Representative Democracy*. New York: Free Press.

Gutmann, Amy, and Dennis Thompson. 2004. *Why Deliberative Democracy*. Princeton, NJ: Princeton University Press.

Hagle, Timothy, and Harold Spaeth. 1993. "Ideological Patterns in the Justices' Voting in the Burger Court's Business Cases." *American Journal of Political Science* 55:492–505.

Hajnal, Zolton. 2009. "Who Loses is American Democracy: Account of Votes Demonstrates the Limited Representation of African Americans." *American Political Science Review* 103:37–57.

Hansen, John Mark. 1991. *Gaining Access: Congress and the Farm Lobby, 1919–1981*. Chicago: University of Chicago Press.

Harris, Fredrick C., Valeria Sinclair-Chapman, and Brian D. McKenzie. 2005. *Countervailing Forces in African-American Civic Activism, 1973–1994*. Cambridge: Cambridge University Press.

Hartley, Thomas, and Bruce Russett. 1992. "Public Opinion and the Common Defense: Who Governs Military Spending in the United States?" *American Political Science Review* 86:905–15.

Hero, Rodney. 1992. *Latinos and the U.S. Political System: Two-Tiered Pluralism*. Philadelphia: Temple University Press.

Hill, Kim Quaile. 1998. "The Policy Agendas of the President and the Mass Public: A Research Validation and Extension." *American Journal of Political Science* 42:1328–34.

Hochschild, Jennifer. 2006. "When Do People Not Protest Unfairness? The Case of Skin Color Discrimination." *Social Research: An International Quarterly* 73:473–98.

Hurwitz, Mark, William Mishler, and Reginald Sheehan. 2004. "The Influence of Public Opinion on Supreme Court Decision-Making." Paper presented at the annual meeting for the American Political Science Association in Chicago, IL on September 2–5, 2004

Hutchings, Vincent, Harwood McClerking, and Guy-Uriel Charles. 2004. "Congressional Representation of Black Interests: Recognizing the Importance of Stability." *Journal of Politics* 66:450–68.

Inglehart, Ronald, and Gabriela Catterberg. 2002. "Trends in Political Action: The Development Trend and the Post-Honeymoon." *Sage* 43:300–18.

Jacobs, Lawrence, and Robert Shapiro. 1994. "Studying Substantive Democracy: Public Opinion, Institutions, and Policymaking." *PS: Political Science and Politics* 27:9–16.

2000. *Politicians Don't Pander: Political Manipulation and the Loss of Democratic Responsiveness*. Chicago, IL: University of Chicago Press.

Jenkins, Craig, and Charles Perrow. 1977. "Insurgency of the Powerless: Farm Worker Movements (1946–1972)." *American Sociological Review* 42:249–68.

Jennings, M. Kent. 1987. "Residues of a Movement: The Aging of the American Protest Generation." *American Political Science Review* 81:367–82.

Johnson, Lyndon. 1965. "Statement By the President on the Situation in Selma." *The American Presidency Project*. http://www.presidency.ucsb.edu/ws/?pid=26802

Kahn, Ronald. 1999. "Institutionalized Norms and Supreme Court Decision-Making: The Rehnquist Court on Privacy and Religion." In *Supreme Court Decision-Making: New Institutionalist Approaches*, ed. Clayton Cornell and Gillman Howard. Chicago: University of Chicago Press.

Kane, Melinda. 2003. "Social Movement Policy Success: Decriminalizing State Sodomy Laws, 1969–1998." *Mobilization: An International Quarterly* 8:313–34.

Kennedy, John F. 1964. John F. Kennedy: 1963: Containing the Public Messages, Speeches, and Statements of the President, January 20 to November 22, 1963. Washington: Government Printing Office.

Kernell, Samuel. 1993. *Going Public: New Strategies of Presidential Leadership*. Washington, DC: CQ Press.

King, Brayden, Keith Bentele, and Sarah Soule. 2007. "Protest and Policymaking: Explaining Fluctuation in Congressional Attention to Rights Issues, 1960–1986." *Social Forces* 86:137–63.

King, Brayden, Marie Cornwall, and Eric Dahlin. 2005. "Winning Woman Suffrage One Step At a Time: Social Movements and the Logic of the Legislative Process." *Social Forces* 86:1211–34.

King, Brayden, and Sarah Soule. 2007. "Social Movements as Extra-Institutional Entrepreneurs: The Effect of Protests on Stock Price Returns." *Administrative Science Quarterly* 52:413.

King, Gary, and Lyn Ragsdale. 1988. *The Elusive Executive: Discovering Statistical Patterns in the Presidency*. Washington, D.C.: Congressional Quarterly Press.

Kitschelt, Herbert. 1986. "Political Opportunity Structures and Political Protest: Anti-Nuclear Movements in Four Democracies." *British Journal of Political Science* 16:57–85.

Klarman, Michael. 2004. *From Jim Crow to Civil Rights: The Supreme Court and the Struggle for Racial Equality*. New York: Oxford University Press.

Klinkner, Philip A., and Rogers M. Smith. 2002. *The Unsteady March: The Rise and Decline of Racial Equality in America*. Chicago: University of Chicago Press.

Kluger, Richard. 1976. *Simple Justice*. New York: Knopf.

Kotz, Nick. 2005. *Judgement Days*. Boston: Houghton Mifflin.

Lawson, Steven F., and Charles M. Payne. 1998. *Debating the Civil Rights Movement, 1945–1968*. Lanham, MD: Rowman & Littlefield.

Lee, Taeku. 2002. *Mobilizing Public Opinion: Black Insurgency and Racial Attitudes in the Civil Rights*. Chicago: University of Chicago Press.

Levin, Henry. 1979. "Education and Earnings of Blacks and the Brown Decision." In *Have We Overcome?: Race Relations Since Brown, 1954–1979*, ed. Michael V. Namorato. Jackson: The University Press of Mississippi.

Lien, Pei-te, M. Margaret Conway, and Janelle Wong. 2004. *The Politics of Asian Americans: Diversity and Community*. Routledge.

Light, Paul Charles. 1982. *The President's Agenda: Domestic Policy Choice From Kennedy to Carter (With Notes on Ronald Reagan*. Baltimore: Johns Hopkins University Press.

Link, Michael. 1995. "Tracking Public Mood in the Supreme Court: Cross-Time Analyses of Criminal Procedure and Civil Rights Case." *Political Research Quarterly* 48:61–78.

Lipsky, Michael. 1968. "Protest as a Political Resource." *American Political Science Review* 62:1144–58.

1970. *Protest in City Politics: Rent Strikes, Housing and the Power of the Poor*. Chicago: Rand McNally.

Logan, Harold. 1978. "U.S. Rights Panel Backs Univ. Affirmative Action." *The Washington Post* A3.

Lohmann, Susanne. 1993. "A Signaling Model of Informative and Manipulative Political Action." *American Political Science Review* 87:319–33.

1995. "A Signaling Model of Competitive Political Pressures." *Economics and Politics* 7:181–206.

Lublin, David. 1997. *The Paradox of Representation*. Princeton, NJ: Princeton University Press.

Luders, Joseph E. 2010. *The Civil Rights Movement and the Logic of Social Change*. Cambridge: Cambridge University Press.

Madison, James. 1787a. "Federalist No. 10: The Utility of the Union as a Safeguard Against Domestic Faction and Insurrection." *Daily Advertiser*

1787b. "Federalist No. 51: The Union as a Safeguard Against Domestic Faction and Insurrection." *New York Daily Advertiser*

Manning, Jennifer E., and Colleen J. Shogan. 2010. "U.S. Congressional Research Service. African American Members of the United States Congress: 1870–2009."

Mansbridge, Jane. 1994. "Politics of Persuasion." In *The Dynamics of American Politics*, ed. Lawrence Dodd and Calvin C. Jillson. Boulder, CO: Westview.

Marable, Manning. 2004. *W. E. B. Du Bois: Black Radical Democrat*. Paradigm Publishers.

Mars, David. 1969. "The Federal Government and Protest." *Annals of the American Academy of Political and Social Science* 382:120–30.

Mayhew, David. 1974. *Congress: The Electoral Connection*. New Haven, CT: Yale University Press.

McAdam, Doug. 1982. *Political Process and the Development of Black Insurgency, 1930–1970*. Chicago: University of Chicago Press.

1983. "Tactical Innovation and the Pace of Insurgency." *American Sociological Review* 48:735–54.

1996. "The Framing Function of Movement Tactics: Strategic Dramaturgy in the American Civil Rights Movement." In *Comparative Perspectives on Social Movements: Political Opportunities, Mobilizing Structures, and Cultural Framings*, ed. Doug McAdam, John McCarthy, and Mayer Zald. Cambridge: Cambridge University Press.

McAdam, Doug, and Yang Su. 2002. "The War At Home: Antiwar Protests and Congressional Voting, 1965 to 1973." *American Sociological Review* 67:696–721.

McAdam, Doug, and Sidney Tarrow. 2010. "Ballots and Barricades: On the Reciprocal Relationship Between Elections and Social Movements." *Perspectives on Politics* 8:529–42.

McAdam, Doug, Sidney Tarrow, and Charles Tilly. 2001. *Dynamics of Contention*. Cambridge: Cambridge University Press.

McCammon, Holly. 1995. "The Politics of Protection: State Minimum Wage and Maximum Hours Laws for Women in the United States, 1870–1930." *The Sociological Quarterly* 36:217–49.

McCammon, Holly, Karen Campbell, Ellen Granberg, and Christine Mowery. 2001. "How Movements Win: Opportunity Structures and the State Women's Suffrage Movements, 1866–1919." *American Sociological Review* 66:49–70.

McCombs, Maxwell, and Jian-Hua Zhu. 1995. "Capacity, Diversity, and Volatility of the Public Agenda: Trends From 1954 to 1994." *The Public Opinion Quarterly* 59:495–525.

McDonald, Laughlin. 1992. "Legislative Responsiveness and the New Southern Politics." In *Controversies in Minority Voting: Voting Rights Act in Perspective*, ed. Bernard Grofman and Chandler Davidson. New York: Brookings Institution.

McGuire, Kevin, and James Stimson. 2004. "The Least Dangerous Branch Revisited: New Evidence on Supreme Court Responsiveness to Public Preferences." *Journal of Politics* 66:1018–35.

Meyer, David, and Suzanne Staggenborg. 1996. "Movement, Countermovements, and the Structure of Political Opportunity." *American Journal of Sociology* 101:1628–60.

Meyer, David, Valerie Jenness, and Helen Ingram. 2005. *Routing the Opposition*. Minneapolis: University of Minnesota Press.

Miller, Warren E., and Donald E. Stokes. 1963. "Constituency Influence in Congress." *American Political Science Review* 57:45–56.

Mishler, William, and Reginald Sheehan. 1993. "The Supreme Court as a Countermajoritarian Institution? The Impact of Public Opinion on Supreme Court Decisions." *The American Political Science Review* 87:87–101.

1996. "Public Opinion, the Attitudinal Model, and Supreme Court Decision Making: A Micro-Analytic Perspective." *Journal of Politics* 58:169–200.

Moe, Terry, and William Howell. 1999. "The Presidential Power of Unilateral Action." *Journal of Law, Economics, and Organization* 15:132–79.

Monroe, Alan. 1998. "Public Opinion and Public Policy, 1980–1993." *The Public Opinion Quarterly* 62:6–28.

Morgan, Thomas. 1980. "A Sense of Commitment and Festivity Marks First Black College Day March." *Washington Post*, A10

Munoz, Carlos. 1989. *Youth, Identity, Power: The Chicano Movement*. London: Verso.

Neier, Aryeh. 1982. *Only Judgment, the Limits of Litigation in Social Change*. Middletown, CT: Wesleyan University Press.

Nelson, Jack. 2003. "Reporting on the Civil Rights Movement." *Nieman Reports* 57.

Neustadt, Richard E. 1991. *Presidential Power and the Modern Presidents*. New York: Free Press.

Newman, Maria. 1992. "After the Riots: Washington At Work; Lawmaker From Riot Zone Insists on a New Role for Black Politicians." *New York Times* http://www.nytimes.com/1992/05/19/us/after-riots-washington-work-lawmaker-riot-zone-insists-new-role-for-black.html?pagewanted=all&src=pm: Accessed on September 11, 2011.

Nixon, Richard. 1969. "Statement on Signing the Bill Establishing the Cabinet Committee on Opportunities for Spanish-Speaking People." *The American Presidency Project*. http://www.presidency.ucsb.edu/ws/?pid=2392

1971. "Annual Message to the Congress on the State of the Union." *The American Presidency Project*. http://www.presidency.ucsb.edu/ws/?pid=9138

Norpoth, Helmut, and Jeffrey Segal. 1994. "Popular Influence on Supreme Court Decisions." *American Political Science Review* 88:711–24.

O'Reilly, Kenneth. 1995. *Nixon's Piano: Presidents and Racial Politics From Washington to Clinton*. New York: The Free Press.

Obama, Barack. 2009. *A More Perfect Union*. Speech presented at the Philadelphia National Constitution Center, Philadelphia, PA

Olzak, Susan, and Sarah Soule. 2009. "Cross-Cutting Influences of Environmental Protest and Legislation." *Social Forces* 88:201–25.

Omatsu, Glenn. 1994. "The 'Four Prisons' and the Movements of Liberation: Asian American Activism From the 1960's to the 1990's." In *The State of Asian America: Activism and Resistance in the 1990's*, ed. Karin Aguilar-San Juan. Boston: South End Press.

Ong, Paul, Edna Bonacich, and Lucie Cheng. 1994. "The Political Economy of Capitalist Restructuring and the New Asian Immigration." In *The New Asian Immigration in Los Angeles and Global Restructuring*, ed. Paul Ong, Edna Bonacich, and Lucie Cheng. Philadelphia: Temple University Press.

Ostrom, Charles, and Dennis Simon. 1988. "The President's Public." *American Political Science Review* 79:334–58.

Overby, Marvin, and Kenneth Cosgrove. 1996. "Unintended Consequences? Racial Redistricting and the Representation of Minority Interests." *Journal of Politics* 58:540–50.

Page, Benjamin, and Robert Shapiro. 1983. "Effects of Public Opinion on Policy." *The American Political Science Review* 77:175–90.

Parker, Christopher S. 2009. *Fighting for Democracy: Black Veterans and the Struggle Against White Supremacy in Postwar South*. Princeton, NJ: Princeton University Press.

Piereson, James E. 1975. "Presidential Popularity and Midterm Voting At Different Electoral Levels." *American Journal of Political Science* 19:683–94.

Pious, Richard. 1979. *The American Presidency*. New York: Basic Books.

Piven, Frances, and Richard Cloward. 1977. *Poor People's Movement: Why They Succeed, Why They Fail*. New York: Pantheon.

Piven, Frances Fox, and Richard Cloward. 1971. *Regulating the Poor: The Functions of Public Welfare*. Vintage.

Polsby, Nelson. 1968. "The Institutionalization of the House of Representatives." *American Political Science Review* 62:144–69.

1984. *Political Innovation in America: The Politics of Policy Initiation*. New Haven, CT: Yale University Press.

Pomper, Gerald. 1989. "The Presidential Election." In *The Election of 1988: Reports and Interpretations*, ed. Gerald Pomper, Ross Baker, Walter Burnham, Barbara Farah, Hershey Margaret, Ethel Klein, and Wilson McWilliams. Chatham, NJ: Chatham House.

Poole, Keith, and Howard Rosenthal. 1997. *A Political-Economic History of Roll Call Voting*. New York: Oxford University Press.

Pritchett, Herman. 1964. "Equal Protection and the Urban Majority." *The American Political Science Review* 58:869–75.

Quadagno, Jill. 1992. "State Transformation and Social Movements: Labor Unions and Racial Conflict in the War on Poverty." *American Sociological Review* 57:616–34.

Ragsdale, Lynn, and John Theis. 1997. "The Institutionalization of the American Presidency, 1924–1992." *American Journal of Political Science* 41:1280–318.

Reed, Adolph. 1986. *The Jesse Jackson Phenomenon: The Crisis of Purpose in Afro-American Politics*. New Haven, CT: Yale University Press.

Reeves, Richard. 1994. *President Kennedy: Profile of Power*. Simon and Schuster.

Rehnquist, William. 1986. "Constitutional Law and Public Opinion." *Suffolk University Law Review* 20:751.

Rich, Wilbur. 2007. *African American Perspectives on Political Science*. Philadelphia: Temple University Press.

Riley, Russell. 1999. *The Presidency and the Politics of Racial Inequality*. New York: Columbia University Press.

Rochon, Thomas. 1998. *Culture Moves*. Princeton, NJ: Princeton University Press.

Rohde, David. 2010. *Political Institutions and Public Choice House Roll-Call Database*. Durham, NC: Duke University.

Rosenberg, Gerald N. 1991. *The Hollow Hope*. Chicago: University of Chicago Press.

Rucht, Dieter. 1999. "The Impact of Environmental Movements in Western Societies." In *How Social Movements Matter*, ed. Marco Giugni, Doug McAdam, and Charles Tilly. Minneapolis: University of Minnesota Press.

Rustin, Bayard. 1965. "From Protest to Politics." *Commentary* 30:25.

Saad, Lydia. 2008. "On King Holiday, a Split Review of Civil Rights Progress." http://www.gallup.com/poll/103828/civil-rights-progress-seen-more.aspx. Accessed October 4, 2010.

Salokar, Rebecca. 1992. *The Solicitor General: The Politics of Law*. Philadelphia: Temple University Press.

Santoro, Wayne. 2002. "The Civil Rights Movement's Struggle for Fair Employment: A 'Dramatic Events-Conventional Politics' Model." *Social Forces* 81:177–206.

Sax, Joseph. 1971. *Defending the Environment: A Strategy for Citizen Action*. New York: Alfred A. Knopf.

Schuman, Howard, Charlotte Steeh, Lawrence Bobo, and Maria Krysan. 1998. *Racial Attitudes in America: Trends and Interpretations*. Cambridge, MA: Harvard University Press.

Scott, James. 1985. *Weapons of the Weak: Everyday Forms of Peasant Resistance*. New Haven, CT: Yale University Press.

Segal, Jeffery. 2009. "Judicial Behavior." In *The Oxford Handbook of Political Science*, ed. Robert E. Goodin. New York: Oxford University Press.

Segal, Jeffrey. 1988. "Amicus Curiae Briefs By the Solicitor General During the Warren and Burger Courts." *Western Political Quarterly* 41:135–44.

Segal, Jeffrey, and Albert Cover. 1989. "Ideological Values and the Votes of U.S. Supreme Court Justices." *The American Political Science Review* 83:557–65.

Segal, Jeffrey, and Harold Spaeth. 1993. *The Supreme Court and the Attitudinal Model*. Cambridge: Cambridge University Press.

2002. *The Supreme Court and the Attitudinal Model Revisited*. Cambridge: Cambridge University Press.

Simon, Dennis, and Charles Ostrom. 1985. "The President and Public Support: A Strategic Perspective." In *The Presidency and Public Policy Making*, ed. George Edwards III, Steven Shull, and Norman Thomas. Pittsburgh: University of Pittsburgh Press.

Sniderman, Paul M. 2000. "Taking Sides: A Fixed Choice Theory of Political Reasoning." In *Elements of Reason: Cognition, Choice, and the Bounds of Rationality*., ed. Arthur Lupia, Mathew McCubbins, and Samuel Popkin. New York: Cambridge University Press.

Snow, David, and Robert Benford. 1988. "Ideology, Frame Resonance, and Participant Mobilization." *International Social Movement Research* 1:197–217.

Sorensen, Theodore. 2005. *Decision-Making in the White House: The Olive Branch or the Arrows*. New York: Columbia University Press.

Soule, Sarah, and Christian Davenport. 2009. "Velvet Glove, Iron Fist Or Even Hand? Protest Policing in the United States, 1960–1990." *Mobilization: An International Quarterly* 14:1–22.

Soule, Sarah, Doug McAdam, John McCarthy, and Yang Su. 1999. "Protest Events: Cause Or Consequence of State Action? The U.S. Women's Movement and Federal Congressional Activities, 1956–1979." *Mobilization: An International Quarterly* 4:239–56.

Soule, Sarah, and Brayden King. 2006. "The Stages of the Policy Process and the Equal Rights Amendment, 1972–1982." *American Journal of Sociology* 111:1871–909.

Soule, Sarah, and Susan Olzak. 2004. "When Do Movements Matter? The Politics of Contingency and the Equal Rights Amendment." *American Sociological Review* 69:473–97.

Spaeth, Harold. 1965. "Jurimetrics and Professor Mendelson: A Troubled Relationship." *The Journal of Politics* 27:875–80.

1999. *United States Supreme Court Judicial Database, 1955–1997*. Ann Arbor, MI: Inter-university Consortium for Political and Social Research.

Spann, Girardeau. 1993. *Race Against the Court*. New York: New York University Press.

Spence, Michael. 1973. "Job Market Signaling." *The Quarterly Journal of Economics* 87:355–74.

Stern, Mark. 1985. "Legislative Responsiveness and the New Southern Politics." In *The Voting Rights Act: Consequences and Implications*, ed. Lorn Foster. New York: Praeger Publishers.

Stimson, James. 1985. "Regression Models in Space and Time: A Statistical Essay." *American Journal of Political Science* 29:914–47.

Stimson, James, Michael MacKuen, and Robert Erikson. 1995. "Dynamic Representation." *American Political Science Review* 89:543–65.

Stimson, James A. 1999. Public Opinion in America: Moods, Cycles, and Swings, Second Edition (Transforming American Politics [Paperback]. Westview Press.

Stolberg, Sheryl Gay, and Marjorie Connelly. 2009. "Obama Is Nudging Views on Race, a Survey Finds." *New York Times*, A1.

Sulkin, Tracy. 2005. *Issue Politics in Congress*. Cambridge: Cambridge University Press.

Swain, Carol. 1993. *Black Faces, Black Interests: The Representation of African Americans in Congress*. Cambridge, MA: Harvard University Press.

Talbert, Jeffery, Bryan Jones, and Frank Baumgartner. 1995. "Nonlegislative Hearings and Policy Change in Congress." *American Journal of Political Science* 39:383–405.

Tanenhaus, Joseph. 1963. "The Supreme Court's Certiorari Jurisdiction: Cue Theory." In *Judicial Decision-Making*, ed. Glendon Schubert. New York: Glencoe Free Press.

Tarrow, Sidney. 1992. "Mentalities, Political Cultures, and Collective Action Frames." In *Frontiers in Social Movement Theory*, ed. Aldon D. Morris and Carol M. Mueller. New Haven, CT: Yale University Press.

1998. *Power in Movement: Social Movements and Contentious Politics*. Cambridge: Cambridge University Press.

Tate, Katherine. 1994. *From Protest to Politics: The New Black Voters in American Elections*. Cambridge, MA: Harvard University Press.

Tauber, Steven. 1998. "On Behalf of the Condemned? The Impact of the NAACP Legal Defense Fund on Capital Punishment Decision Making in the U.S. Courts of Appeals." *Political Research Quarterly* 51:191–219.

1999. "The NAACP Legal Dense Fund and the U.S. Supreme Court's Racial Discrimination Decision Making." *Social Science Quarterly* 80:325–40.

Tilly, Charles. 2006. *Regimes and Repertoires*. Chicago: University of Chicago Press.

Tong, Lorraine H. 2011. "U.S. Congressional Research Service. Asian Pacific Americans in the United States Congress: 1870–2009." *Congressional Research Service Report.* http://www.fas.org/sgp/crs/misc/97-398.pdf. Accessed on May 25, 2011.

Tushnet, Mark. 1987. *The NAACP's Legal Strategy Against Segregated Education*. Chapel Hill: University of North Carolina Press.

Ulmer, Sidney. 1970. "Dissent Behavior and the Social Background of Supreme Court Justices." *Journal of Politics* 32:580–98.

1973. "The Longitudinal Behavior of Hugo Lafayette Black: Parabolic Support for Civil Liberties, 1937–1971." *Florida State University Law Review* 1:131–53.

Ulmer, Sidney, and Michael Thompson. 1981. "Supreme Court Support for Black Litigants: A Comparison of the Warren and Burger Courts." In *In Courts, Law and Judicial Processes*, ed. Sidney Ulmer. New York: The Free Press.

Ulmer, Sidney, William Hintze, and Louise Kirklosy. 1972. "The Decision to Grant Certiorari: Further Consideration of Cue Theory." *Law and Society Review* 6:637–43.

Verba, Sidney, and Norman Nie. 1972. *Participation in America: Political Democracy and Social Equality*. New York: Harper and Row.

Wasby, Stephen L., Anthony A. D'Amato, and Rosemary Metrailer. 1977. *Desegregation From Brown to Alexander: An Exploration of*

Supreme Court Strategies. Carbondale: Southern Illinois University Press.

Wei, William. 1993. *The Asian American Movement*. Philadelphia: Temple University Press.

Weiner, Melissa. 2009. "Elite Versus Grassroots: Disjunctures Between Parents' and Civil Rights Organizations' Demands for New York City's Public Schools." *The Sociological Quarterly* 50:89–119.

Welch, Susan. 1975. "The Impact of Urban Riots on Urban Expenditures." *American Political Science Review* 19:741–60.

Whitaker, Joseph. 1977. "1600 Students Protest Bakke Case." *New York Times*, C1.

Whitby, Kenny J. 1987. "Measuring Congressional Responsiveness to the Policy Interests of Black Constituents." *Social Science Quarterly* 68:367–77.

1997. *The Color of Representation: Congressional Behavior and Black Interests*. Ann Arbor: The University of Michigan Press.

2002. "Bill Sponsorship and Intraracial Voting Among African American Representatives." *American Politics Research* 30:93–109.

Whitby, Kenny J., and Franklin Gilliam, Jr. 1991. "A Longitudinal Analysis of Competing Explanations for the Transformation of Southern Congressional Politics." *Journal of Politics* 53:504–18.

Williams, Juan. 1998. *Thurgood Marshall: American Revolutionary*. New York: Times Books.

Wlezien, Christopher. 2004. "Patterns of Representation: Dynamics of Public Preferences and Policy." *Journal of Politics* 66:1–24.

Woodward, Vann. 1976. *The Strange Career of Jim Crow*, 3rd Ed. New York: Oxford University Press.

Woolley, John T., and Gerhard Peters. 2008. "The American Presidency Project." http://www.presidency.ucsb.edu/. Accessed July 30, 2008.

World Values Survey Association. 2009. "World Values Survey Aggregated 1981–2008 Official Aggregate." http://www.wvsevsdb.com/wvs/WVSData.jsp

Zaller, John. 1992. *The Nature and Origins of Mass Opinion*. Cambridge: Cambridge University Press.

Index

Titles in the Series *(continued from page iii)*

Jack A. Goldstone, editor, *States, Parties, and Social Movements*

Tamara Kay, *NAFTA and the Politics of Labor Transnationalism*

Joseph Luders, *The Civil Rights Movement and the Logic of Social Change*

Doug McAdam and Hilary Boudet, *Putting Social Movements in Their Place: Explaining Opposition to Energy Projects in the United States, 2000–2005*

Doug McAdam, Sidney Tarrow, and Charles Tilly, *Dynamics of Contention*

Holly J. McCammon, *The U.S. Women's Jury Movements and Strategic Adaptation: A More Just Verdict*

Sharon Nepstad, *War Resistance and the Plowshares Movement*

Kevin J. O'Brien and Lianjiang Li, *Rightful Resistance in Rural China*

Silvia Pedraza, *Political Disaffection in Cuba's Revolution and Exodus*

Eduardo Silva, *Challenging Neoliberalism in Latin America*

Sarah Soule, *Contention and Corporate Social Responsibility*

Yang Su, *Collective Killings in Rural China during the Cultural Revolution*

Sidney Tarrow, *The New Transnational Activism*

Ralph Thaxton, Jr., *Catastrophe and Contention in Rural China: Mao's Great Leap Forward Famine and the Origins of Righteous Resistance in Da Fo Village*

Charles Tilly, *Contentious Performances*

Charles Tilly, *The Politics of Collective Violence*

Charles Tilly, *Contention and Democracy in Europe, 1650–2000*

Marisa von Bülow, *Building Transnational Networks: Civil Society and the Politics of Trade in the Americas*

Lesley J. Wood, *Direct Action, Deliberation, and Diffusion: Collective Action after the WTO Protests in Seattle*

Stuart A. Wright, *Patriots, Politics, and the Oklahoma City Bombing*

Deborah Yashar, *Contesting Citizenship in Latin America: The Rise of Indigenous Movements and the Postliberal Challenge*

Andrew Yeo, *Activists, Alliances, and Anti–U.S. Base Protests*